The use of counselling
IN THE EMERGENCY SERVICES

The use of counselling skills
IN THE EMERGENCY SERVICES

Angela Hetherington

Open University Press
Buckingham • Philadelphia

Open University Press
Celtic Court
22 Ballmoor
Buckingham
MK18 1XW

email: enquiries@openup.co.uk
world wide web: www.openup.co.uk

and
325 Chestnut Street
Philadelphia, PA 19106, USA

First Published 2001

A catalogue record of this book is available from the British Library

ISBN   0 335 20060 5 (pb)   0 335 20061 3 (hb)

Library of Congress Cataloging-in-Publication Data
Hetherington, Angela, 1953–
    The use of counselling skills in the emergency services / Angela
Hetherington.
        p. cm.
    Includes bibliographical references and index.
    ISBN 0–335–20061–3 – ISBN 0–335–20060–5 (pbk.)
    1. Emergency medical services.   2. First aid in illness and injury.
3. Counseling.   I. Title.
RA 645.5 .H47 2001
616.02′5–dc21   00-060678

Typeset by Graphicraft Limited, Hong Kong
Printed in Great Britain by St Edmundsbury Press Ltd,
Bury St Edmunds, Suffolk

To Tamarind and Imogen

Contents

Acknowledgements

Much of the illustrative material in the text is derived from work conducted originally with the emergency services through the Home Office. In respect of this I would like to thank David Webb and Sandra Wilkinson, who promoted this research. I am also grateful to the emergency service personnel who candidly conveyed to me their thoughts and feelings about their working lives. I thank Michael Jacobs for his direction and constructive editing of the text, Jon Slack for his critical reading of the original draft and Philip Sanders for his support in the completion of the text. I am especially grateful to Karen Peake, who has worked alongside me in the production of the book, and whose assistance I have very much appreciated. My thanks also to my two daughters, Imogen for help with the referencing of the text, and Tamarind for the original cover illustration.

Preface

This book seeks to apply the theoretical rationale for counselling skills to the practical nature of emergency service work. With this intention, much of the discussion on the practical use of counselling skills by emergency service professionals is based on research into the stress and trauma of emergency service work (Hetherington 1993; Hetherington and Munro 1996). The responses of a broad sample of emergency service professionals involved in that research are referred to throughout the book, either in the form of narrative cases or as direct quotes. Specific details have been changed to protect anonymity. The views expressed by emergency personnel, like the associated research, may change in relation to new developments, and as such may create as much argument as they may do agreement. The combination of continued debate and informed practice form the medium for continued learning about the appropriate use of counselling skills.

The book is intended primarily to promote discussion on the effective use of counselling skills both when dealing with the public and in the workplace with fellow colleagues. The book addresses issues experienced by the fire service, police service, accident and emergency and ambulance personnel in their daily work. The material is also of relevance to disaster workers and to the voluntary emergency services such as the British Red Cross. Although caution should be used in applying the experiences of any one professional group to those of another, the commonality of certain aspects of the job such as working with traumatic incidents and their aftermath allows some generalization.

The nature of emergency service work can involve regular exposure of personnel to traumatic incidents. This requires emergency service professionals to understand and to manage the post traumatic reactions of individuals with whom they are dealing. Equally their frequent exposure to traumatic incidents can render professionals themselves vulnerable to post traumatic stress reactions. For this reason, the specific emotional and psychological sequelae of traumatic experiences together with appropriate individual and organizational interventions are considered in more depth.

It is important that counselling skills are practised in full knowledge of the individual and organizational responsibilities for their use. Thus the trained use of counselling skills by personnel in their various roles as professionals, peers and managers is discussed within a legal and professional perspective. The more detailed information on the ethical and legal implications in the use of counselling skills is by its nature bound by theory and can be used for reference when required.

The book is written from a female perspective, which will have influenced the views expressed; equally it will have been influenced by being written from a psychologist's viewpoint and not from an emergency service employee's perspective. This may lead to debate in itself about some of the issues raised; however, the text is not intended to be prescriptive but to raise issues for further discussion.

Chapter 1

Counselling skills in the context of the emergency services

The attraction to the job

Adrenalin's flowing, tension's high, everyone's geared up ready to fly into action to manage the emergency situation. It's everything we've been trained for, the whole team. At times like this no one remembers the failed rescues, no one thinks of the aftermath, the personal price, only the chance of doing it well.

Working for the emergency services is a challenging and potentially highly rewarding vocation. Yet by the nature of the job it is one of the most stressful occupations. Police officers, firefighters, disaster workers, medical, ambulance and voluntary emergency personnel all contend with considerable stress as a result of their responsibility for the life and safety of others. The cumulative stress and the trauma of the job can have damaging effects on their personal and professional lives. Yet the unpredictability of the amount and type of work in the emergency services, even if sources of stress, are also found to be attractive features of the job to certain personality dispositions.

Research has shown that the people who are attracted to a career with inherent powerful stressors have very different personalities from the average person who holds a far less risky or demanding job (Mitchell and Bray 1990). Emergency professionals tend to have high levels of commitment, challenge and control and are more resilient to stress (Hetherington 1993). They find the job rewarding and set high personal standards, but experience considerable anguish in the event of failure. Emergency personnel are more likely to be outgoing and are motivated by internal factors such as the satisfaction of the job and a personal sense of competence. They do not like deferred gratification and are more easily bored. They are frequently action oriented, task oriented and quicker to make decisions and to take risks. Emergency personnel lay themselves open to dangers associated with exposure to disease, violence, mutilation and death. They are motivated to assist and to rescue others and to intervene actively in disputes, conflicts, disasters and potentially dangerous situations.

The nature of the job

I recall nearly all of the accidents I've attended vividly. Some have upset me deeply at the time but it's important to shut off so you can help the people involved. I try to avoid looking back at an accident because if I think about it too long I remember the family the victim may have left and the grief they must feel. I have been adversely affected by these accidents but the change in me has been gradual therefore it's difficult to describe exactly how I've changed. I have grown accustomed to death and to fear.

This quote by a senior ranking emergency service employee highlights the indelible impact that emergencies have on those who respond to them and raises the question of why and how they manage such events.

Human problems are universal, as is an inclination to help others experiencing difficulties. For those involved in traumatic incidents, their reactions to the event are disturbing in themselves. To manage traumatized individuals requires fundamental skills to diffuse the emotions of those involved sufficiently to allow them to cope more readily with their immediate situation.

The skills involved in these situations are remarkably similar. They are core human skills which can be applied to most situations. When used effectively they are at times barely discernible and enable the professionals to fulfil their primary role.

Yet when used badly, they can compound the problem for both the individuals concerned and for the professionals in the execution of their duties.

Counselling skills may be actively employed within the emergency profession in a variety of forms. These include the use of skills in the interface with the public, with peers at work, and in a supervisory or management capacity. Each of these applications ultimately influences the internal organizational culture and its external public image.

The use of counselling skills in the job

Never having come across A and E [accident and emergency] work, where the psychological abuse of staff is commonplace, it was a shock knowing how to deal with it. Experience and a counselling course has given me a lot of help and guidance in dealing with these things, and with my own stress.

Attitudes towards authority have changed considerably over the years. No longer can an emergency service worker rely on their role or their status as a professional to command respect. For the police, achieving public compliance with the law is increasingly dependent on allaying conflict and negotiating acceptable behaviour. Forging a relationship with an individual, through sensitivity and the appropriate use of social skills, can be an effective way of influencing their behaviour and resolving disputes. Equally, when members of the public are emotionally overwhelmed by a traumatic event, effective interpersonal interaction by an emergency service worker can help to restore a sense of control to the situation, and manage some of the associated mental anguish for those involved. Creating an immediate rapport with an individual in a state of high emotion, containing their feelings and striving to achieve a useful outcome, entails a considerable amount of interpersonal skill and experience. These abilities can be considered to be core counselling skills.

Training in counselling skills provides the emergency services with a powerful tool in the dynamics of their interaction with the public. The use of such skills in the job can be mutually rewarding, providing the emergency service professional with a sense of fulfilment and engendering in the public an appreciation for the support proffered. Frequently, the competent use of trained skills may at times be the only reward available for the emergency service in the face of public abuse, disaster or devastation. The sometimes ungratifying nature of police work is reflected in the following road traffic patrol officer's expressions of frustrations with the job:

> The root cause of fatal accidents is often selfishness and disregard for the lives and welfare of others. These people vent their frustration and rage on innocent victims. They are the ones who usually survive, leaving the victim's family with the pain for their loss, and their anger at us for not bringing the guilty party to justice. Even if they are brought to book, the odds seem stacked in their favour and a pitifully inadequate sentence is passed on them.

The following situation was reported by a student in training who felt at the time unable to cope with the situation. Such situations inevitably require experience to allow the professional to become resilient to the more distressing elements of the event. The trained use of counselling skills can not only help those immediately involved in the situation to come to terms with the disturbing event but equally enable the professional to feel that their support has been worthwhile.

> An old man was brought into A and E, saying that he was dying. He was referred on to the surgical on-call team who decided, considering his age and quality of life, that no surgical intervention should be taken. His wife was brought in. As he said Goodbye and thanked her for everything, he suddenly deteriorated. I felt overwhelmed and had to leave. A senior nurse stayed with him and his wife until he died.

This illustration also highlights the strengths and limitations of counselling skills. The man's death was inevitable. Yet the ability of the nurse to remain with the couple and to use her presence skilfully would have provided support to both the man and his wife. Many devastating life situations of this kind can be managed more effectively through the use of counselling skills. Events which the emergency services respond to are primarily crises in the lives of those concerned. They also involve life events which require problem solving or interpersonal skills of the individuals involved. These situations require counselling skills of the professional if the situation is to achieve a more positive outcome. The outcome may be immediately evident. More likely, it will be longer term. People learn from modelled behaviour and from the cumulative effects of their experience. The supportive intervention from a figure of authority may have considerable effects on an individual whose experience of respect from others has been limited.

Egan (1986) makes the point that in the majority of cases, helping skills, including counselling skills, are provided by people who are not counsellors. Yet in the case of the emergency services, the dual roles can incur immediate conflict. For example, police officers who are effectively using counselling skills primarily have responsibility for upholding the law. Counselling skills may in fact enable them to conduct their law enforcement duties more successfully; but if these fail, police officers must ultimately act to enforce the law. For this reason, confidentiality emerges as a pivotal issue in the practice of counselling skills in the emergency services. Where the use of counselling skills occurs within a network of conflicting accountabilities, it is important that the limits to confidentiality are clear to the professional and conveyed unambiguously to the individual being supported.

Formal peer support in the workplace

In addition to using counselling skills effectively as part of their jobs, individuals are increasingly required to employ them to the benefit of their colleagues in the form of peer support. The emergency service, being in part a helping profession, may be considered to have the necessary skills and expertise required for people to help each other. Such an assumption is contested by Feltham (1997), who argues that it could be automatically assumed that an occupation that is part of a 'people profession' necessarily means that it is equipped to provide counselling for its own staff. The emergency services, however, delineate between counselling for staff and peer support for staff. Employees requiring counselling are referred to trained counsellors, specialists who are either internal or external to the organization as required. Peers provide a more readily available and formal collegiate support system founded on the commonality of their experience within the profession, their motivation to help and their training in counselling skills. Their expertise lies in their knowing the limitations of their skills, the boundaries of their role, and enabling the employee to access professional help. Untrained, informal support by well-intentioned colleagues can unwittingly risk compounding an employee's difficulties. The appreciation of support from peers is reflected in a senior nurse's reaction to an 8-year-old girl's accidental death:

> Three of the staff involved had daughters of the same age. After two weeks of mutual support, we were able to talk about it without feeling distraught. Support came from within the department. We all felt that counsellors couldn't possibly know or understand how we felt.

The use of counselling skills in management

The skills of counselling are not only central to effective interpersonal interaction but equally rudimentary to the dynamics of an organization. Listening, a core counselling skill, can be fundamental to an organization's competence and success, forming the basis for good human relations and, in particular, employee and customer relations. Failure to listen and to attend to others cultivates poor communication patterns and unaddressed workplace problems; it also results in employee and customer dissatisfaction. When employers listen to the difficulties experienced by employees, they are effectively relieving them of their preoccupations with their own problem and, at the same time, modelling sound listening skills for use with the public. The following opinion was expressed in frustration by an emergency service worker who was aware of the incongruence between the way in which management seemingly responded to his difficulty and the interface he sought to achieve with the public:

I remember a particular fatality of a baby which, as a new parent, upset me. The supervisor told me to 'get on with it' and not to get emotionally involved. How can we remain human and close to the community if we strive to behave in a way which portrays us not to have feelings in common with members of the public. What can be so wrong at such a time in showing emotion?

Good interpersonal interactions with the workforce enable supervisory staff to remain sensitive to issues such as the employee's experience in the job and current life events, and responsive to the individual's personal interpretation of the incident. What has become commonplace to a seasoned employee may be a shattering experience to another for a variety of unavoidable reasons. Yet in times of trauma when individuals may be more sensitive to negative evaluation, words of criticism can be taken to heart and remain with the individual through the years to come. Counselling training can raise awareness of such issues, promoting a greater understanding of the power of the word and its effect on an individual's psychological well-being and workplace performance.

Organizational implications

There are further benefits to be gained from training in counselling skills. Jarvie and Matthews (1989) list personal development, good communication, high motivation, a high performance team, mutual responsibility and synergy as some of the useful outcomes of skills training. Such assets can benefit the working environment of the organization if given due regard by management and fostered within the structure of the organization (Martin 1997). For example, training in counselling skills within the organization enhances interpersonal skills, improving communication and interaction generally. Research further suggests that there is significant transferability of counselling skills to other specific areas of management, such as appraisal, interviewing and discipline. Given the diversity of applications of counselling skills in the organization, it becomes imperative that individuals trained to fulfil a peer support role are able to distinguish between related activities such as mentoring, advising and appraising (Pickard 1993).

When counselling skills are employed for use within the organization with fellow employees, this can transform its culture. Pearce (1989) notes that the use of counselling skills in the workplace can act as a powerful tool for organizational change and development. McDonald (1991) highlights the reciprocity inherent in the counselling process, reflecting a partnership relationship between client and provider which significantly impacts on the fabric of a successful organization. Partnership is negotiated through communication. Communication is effected through focused and sincere attention to the employee. As much of managerial time is engaged in oral communication, the importance of the quality cannot be underestimated (Hughes 1991). A senior A and E nurse commented on her feelings of exclusion from internal communications within the organization, which is entwined, in her experience, with interpersonal conflicts:

> Lots of our department's stress is caused by personality
> clashes and lack of communication from higher
> management. Changes just happen. There is no
> discussion. You are just expected to get on with it.

This clearly undermines her sense of authority and feelings of value to the organization. The timely use of counselling skills by management to address the issues associated with change and to resolve interpersonal conflict can in the long term be cost effective. At the very least, counselling skills can be instrumental in diffusing the anger and distress generated by the shared working environment as opposed to fostering discontent towards the organization over the longer term. Appropriate interventions by senior management can effectively cascade through the organization, providing models of behaviour which are readily adopted. The absence of assistance for employees who require support as a result of their experiences on the job can be a missed opportunity for an organization to forge a reciprocal relationship with those who work for it. Whether a problem is work related or personal, if it has become disturbing to the employee it can impede their judgement, morale or performance, and ultimately impact on organizational effectiveness. Failing to support employees in the execution of their jobs may incur feelings of resentment and anger towards the employer which can interfere with their commitment to the organization. For example, a police officer reported an incident early in his career:

> A car carrying a family of four had collided head on with another vehicle. Passers-by had pulled the children to safety. The smouldering bodies of both parents, burned to death, were still in situ in the vehicle. There's little or no support in the job. The only thing that matters is that you turn up for work the next day.

Although there are indications that the incorporation of counselling skills training into an organization can positively change the organizational ethos, this is not necessarily the case. Argyris and Schon (1984) stress the difference between an organization's 'espoused theory' and its 'theory in use'. The expectation that counselling values may reach the core of an organization and transform its fundamental values may be some way yet from realization. In fact the formal inclusion of counselling support can legitimize stress as a natural and universal product of the job with which the employee must contend, raising the issue of organizational responsibility.

Organizational responsibility

While peer support programmes and professional counselling services for employees can be considered to be effective in moderating the deleterious effects of work-related stress, they can also serve to absolve the employer of responsibility for the source of work-related stress. Newton (1995) is particularly critical of stress management programmes and employee support programmes. He argues that employees' grievances and difficulties are construed as individual concerns as opposed to the collectively justifiable reaction to inadequate working conditions that they might well be. He suggests that staff are subtly manoeuvred into interpreting work-related problems as their own individual responsibility, not as collective concerns. This analysis suggests that the organization benefits from supportive interventions because they reinforce the notion that emotion and discontentment are inappropriate in the workplace.

Feltham (1997: 249) proposes that many organizations could be considered to 'abuse their employees' moral rights' by purporting how they should dress, when they may take coffee, lunch and holiday breaks, and ultimately where they take their problems. Conversely, Plas and Hoover-Dempsey (1988) promote the view that emotions are a part of organizational life and as such should be accepted rather than counselled. This perspective may be adopted successfully by organizations which actively decide to change the work ethos so that feelings and thoughts emanating from work-related events can be openly expressed, rather than contained before being taken to a counsellor. This legitimization of occupational stress can perhaps be most effectively facilitated and catered for in the workplace in the form of systematic staff debriefings. However, fundamental to any workplace policy on stress management must be an organizational willingness to combat the sources of occupational stress which are the result of the organizational structure, practices and working culture.

Essentially, the trained use of counselling skills can serve to facilitate and enhance the routine work of the emergency services, both in the interface with the public and in the relationships among staff. At the same time, they can permeate the culture of the organization to promote interpersonal effectiveness and a healthier working environment. The core features involved in the effective practice of counselling skills in the workplace are considered in the next chapter.

Chapter 2

Issues in the use of counselling skills

Patients with large burns are often difficult to treat because we know they are likely to die. They are usually conscious and distressed. Nothing prepares a relative for how horrific a burnt patient looks. Mostly all of our interactions with the family are comprised of using counselling skills to make the situation more manageable for the patient and their family during the ongoing treatment.

In the emergency services, counselling skills are employed instinctively. In many instances, they are the only tool available to manage in an otherwise devastating situation. The use of counselling skills, constantly modified by experience and exposure to traumatic incidents, is an intrinsic and significant aspect of the role of the emergency service professional. In themselves, they can become a powerful tool when forged with the role and authority of the professional, and as such they must be practiced according to recognized professional codes of practice. Deviation from these codes can incur professional and legal penalties. Central to the proficient use of counselling skills is an appreciation of their distinction from counselling.

The nature of counselling skills

The British Association of Counselling (BAC) produce a detailed code of ethics and conduct specifically related to the use of counselling skills within a primary profession such as the emergency services. They are designed to apply to professionals for whom counselling skills are used to facilitate a primary role. Within the *Code of Ethics and Practice for Counselling Skills* (BAC 1989: B.1.1) they clearly delineate between counselling and counselling skills, stating that, 'what distinguishes the use of counselling skills' from counselling are 'the intentions of the user, which is to enhance the performance of their functional role'. More specifically, in *Guidelines for Those Using Counselling Skills in their Work*, they go on to identify three conditions which constitute the professional use of counselling skills:

- *when* there is intentional use of specific interpersonal skills which reflect the values of counselling
- *and* when the practitioner's primary role (e.g. nurse, tutor, line manager, social worker, personnel officer, helper) is enhanced without being changed
- *and* when the client perceives the practitioner as acting within their primary professional or/caring role which is *not* that of being a counsellor.

(British Association of Counselling 1998: 1)

Newby (1983), in an early article on the subject, suggested that the distinction between 'counselling' and 'counselling skills' is useful because it delineates between the process of the counselling relationship and the skills component of the interaction. While the formation of a relationship is central to professional counselling, in analysing the underlying dynamics and generating insight to the individual's functioning, it is not essential in the effective use of counselling skills. For emergency service workers, the use of skills serves to facilitate their primary role. The formation of a relationship may be counter-productive to the professional's primary function or incongruent with their role at that time; for instance, where a professional is acting in such a way as to achieve the individual's safety, but having achieved it, must take whatever action is necessary in the interests of others. The following incident illustrates the dual role of the medic successfully employing counselling skills while achieving his primary goal to save the lives of those injured and to prevent risk of harm to others. Under such circumstances, where there may be a significant difference in the values of each party, it may feel incongruent for a relationship to be created.

> I talked to the youth as I treated him in an effort to calm the situation and gain his cooperation, knowing that once he was treated he would be arrested for grievous

bodily harm at least. Next door we were also fighting to save the life of his victim. You can't let the justice of the event interfere with you doing your job.

For counselling skills to be a valuable use of the professional's time, they must achieve a fruitful outcome. Their use must enable emergency service workers to carry out their primary role. They must render the situation more manageable for both the professional and for the individual involved. This outcome, while primarily dependent on the ability and training of the professional, is equally determined by the individuals with whom the skills are used. The successful use of counselling skills will be influenced by the receptivity and cooperation of the individual being helped.

The foundations for counselling skills

The greatest job satisfaction came from supporting the parents of a 4-year-old girl brought in dead to A and E. I had already done research on child deaths and felt informed in providing help. Support from peers was very helpful. The parents later wrote to me, thanking me for the things I had said to them.

This incident was reported by an emergency nurse. She had also described feeling upset by the event but the enduring image for her was the difference which she had made to the parents in their experience of an overwhelming event. She had experienced a sense of competence derived from the effective use of skills and a specialist knowledge base which she could draw upon. The constructive use of counselling skills in this instance also allowed her to reframe a devastating event in the context of the positive support she was able to provide. The form of skills used in this example combined informative and crisis counselling.

Supportive counselling

Counselling skills may be used to provide psychological support in crisis or emotional distress. They may also be used in the course of providing information. In the main, supportive counselling at times of emotional distress involves the use of counselling skills in response to the feelings expressed by an individual in response to a particular event. The specific counselling skills used varies according to the nature of the incident, and the extent of the distress being experienced. For instance, in the event of an immediate crisis, non-verbal communication becomes naturally redundant. At such times, an individual may have difficulty in processing any communications clearly. The skills most commonly employed are listening, attending and containing. Many of the incidents with which the emergency service professional deals involve the use of counselling skills both in a supportive and informative mode.

Informative counselling

Informative counselling allows the professional to offer information to the individual which will contribute to their psychological well-being. It should be based on the expert information available to the professional which is outside the experience of the individual concerned. In emergency service work, offering information is often necessary in enabling the individual to take appropriate action in circumstances which are beyond their experience and at times in which they may be less able to think clearly. On occasions, emergency professionals may need to offer information of an educational form, based on their specialist knowledge. For instance, an emergency doctor may provide information on alternative options of medical intervention and their implications to the life of the individual. An emergency professional may offer information at the appropriate time on Sudden Infant Death Syndrome, which may help to allay some of the guilt and self-doubt the parents may experience.

Knowledge base

A sound knowledge base is fundamental to the proficient practice of counselling skills. Skills refers to the practical ability to deliver services. Any successful application of skills is based on a working knowledge of the underlying theory (Egan 1998). Many of these theories are founded on experience and already form an integral part of the professional's current working knowledge. Experience informed by theory can cultivate an applied understanding that enables the professional successfully to use counselling skills in the course of their work. Those areas which may be of value to the professional wishing to extend their working knowledge of human behaviour are:

- a fundamental knowledge of applied developmental psychology, how people react differently according to their age, culture, religion, sexual orientation and socio-economic status
- an understanding of the principles of cognitive psychology, how people think, perceive and make sense of the world about them and the actions of others towards them
- an understanding of the underlying principles of social psychology, group development, interpersonal interaction, nonverbal behaviour, influence, conflict and negotiating behaviour, relationship formation
- a working knowledge of personality theory, individual differences in learning and behaving, individual motivation, underlying dimensions of personality such as extroversion, introversion and neuroticism
- an awareness of abnormal psychology as it is manifested in offending behaviour or psychological difficulties in normal functioning.

The value of a systematic body of knowledge such as is available through psychology is that it enables a professional interpretation of the actions of others. The information available from the behaviour displayed may appear limited, yet further assumptions can be made, based on a knowledge of the underlying influences. This in itself allows the professional to act with insight, to test out assumptions and to moderate their interactions according to the responses they engender in the other. While a sound knowledge base facilitates the use of counselling skills, the individual must have the capacity to apply the knowledge in a systematic and versatile manner to achieve results (McLeod 1998).

Cultural diversity

Cultural diversity is a central issue in the practice of counselling skills within the emergency services. Emergency professionals are in a position to exercise a significant and powerful authority. Within each of the emergency services this power is further compounded by the significance of gender biases among the respective sets of personnel. The implications of the power imbalance on the perceptions of members of the public must be borne in mind, together with their conscious and unconscious significance to the professional.

The use of counselling skills by professionals in their respective roles must be informed by an awareness of cultural difference. Differences in non-verbal behaviour, fundamental values, social norms of behaviour and family structure will inevitably influence the nature of the individual's reactions to the professional. Thus, for emergency service personnel, a working knowledge of the broad characteristics, needs and behaviours of the populations whom they serve – colour, age, gender, religion, special needs – is paramount in the appropriate and competent use of counselling skills. (See Walker 1990 and Lago 1996 for further discussion of gender and cultural variables.)

However, while an appreciation of cultural difference can enhance the use of counselling skills, a greater awareness of group norms can also lead to stereotyping. A fundamental premise of social psychology is that there are as many differences, and sometimes more, within groups as between groups (see Weinrach and Thomas 1996 for a broader discussion of these issues). It is important that professionals adjust any preconceived perceptions of cultural norms in response to feedback from their interactions with individuals. Counselling skills can be rendered ineffective by the inappropriate projection of assumptions and stereotypes of group membership on to individuals.

Transference and counter-transference

Transference and counter-transference refer to the ways in which an individual's responses to current relationships are influenced by patterns of reactions from the past (Jacobs 1999). Individuals tend to respond to significant others in their life in the ways in which they did as children to parental figures. An encounter with an emergency professional may be brief, yet it is often at times of high anxiety, anger or distress in which the presence of a more powerful other can generate feelings akin to those experienced as a child. The role the professional fills during such an intense experience, as either an authority figure or rescuer, can cause the working relationship to be significantly distorted by transference. The active use of counselling skills will also serve to distort the individual's perception of the professional. This combination of factors can cause an individual to experience strong feelings of dependency or closeness, and to imbue the professional with idealized attributes. These feelings, however, are a product of the situation and the individual's temporary state of mind. They are the individual's response to the role the professional fills and the individual's transient neediness for protection or safety. These feelings are unlikely to persist beyond the event other than in fantasy.

Transference describes feelings precipitated in the individual by the professional; counter-transference refers to the feelings stimulated in the professional through their interaction with the individual. Feelings of counter-transference can be a direct response to the individual's feelings towards the professional or can be generated by the professional's own past. Distinguishing between feelings based on reality and those founded on transference is not always clear, particularly in brief focused interactions in the context of emergency service work. The following case suggests the emergence of feelings of both transference and counter-transference in a rescue operation:

> The young woman had been trapped for some time under the rubble of a collapsed building. By the time the fire officer arrived, she had become resigned to possibly not being discovered in time. The officer provided immediate comfort, staying near her and relating closely to her throughout the rescue operation. She began to talk of her boyfriend, his lack of care for her. In describing how he was aggressive and constantly critical of her, she became further upset. The officer actively redirected the conversation on to different aspects of her life to

maintain their interaction on a caring but professional level. Yet he found that after the event, she played on his mind. Outside of his role as a fire officer, he had felt attracted to her vulnerability, and to her need of him.

Often events stay in mind due to their traumatic nature. These are usually highly visual memories frozen in time and relate only to the specific event. If thoughts and fantasies of particular individuals live on after a short encounter it is likely that these are founded on relationships from the past. In the previous example, it is likely that transference and counter-transference feelings were generated in both parties by the intensity of the situation. The officer, recognizing the woman's underlying vulner-ability and her rapid bonding with him, managed her feelings effectively at an appropriate level. While responding in a profes-sional manner, he was still left with counter-transference feelings towards her which went beyond the rescue. For the emergency service professional, acknowledging these feelings and recognizing them as context dependent can promote a quicker recovery from residual feelings of the encounter. Equally, unlike counselling where abstinence of interaction on the part of the counsellor promotes feelings of transference, the active and focused role of the professional allows reality to intrude on transference feel-ings, and anchor the interaction in the present.

Supervision in the use of counselling skills

The use of counselling skills is informed by a working knowledge of the psychology of an individual, and the principles of human interaction. Yet the successful practice of counselling skills is constantly modified by experience. This ongoing practice of adapt-ing skills in the course of their use is fundamental to the learning process. A supervisor can be a most valuable means of continu-ing to learn and refine skills, while allowing their practice to be continually open to external constructive evaluation (Hawkins and Shohet 2000). For emergency service professionals, using coun-selling skills in the execution of their primary roles, supervision may be provided in the form of regular debriefings with supervisory staff. In the case of peer support, involving the prolonged and systematic use of counselling skills, the supervision would be provided formally by a qualified professional. This is often resourced through the welfare department, senior qualified member of staff or a private consultant.

The process of supervision ensures that counselling skills are used safely in accordance with the professional code of ethics. It provides protection both to the recipient and to the user. In addition, it enables the professional to diffuse the feelings and thoughts associated with the active use of counselling skills. This is particularly salient in the course of providing peer support in which the nature of the problems presented may cause the professional to identify more closely with those concerned, and equally to burn out more rapidly. In the case of peer support, the supervisor fulfils the function of ensuring that the professional is not being accessed excessively and that their own well-being is being given appropriate regard. One police officer speaks of the value derived from informal supervision:

> You can never adjust to the death of a child or the
> young parents of a child. The worst part of the job is
> having to tell the bereaved relatives. Nothing can take
> away the immediate experience of anguish and distress
> in these events, but your feelings can't stop you doing
> a professional job. You know that the images of your
> breaking the news will stay with the people for some
> time to come. It's only after the event that there can be
> a release of feelings in talking about your sorrows with
> a colleague or with the sergeant.

This illustration suggests the availability within the organization of peer support. In part this appears to be promoted by the organizational culture implied by the officer's acceptance of the normality of his responses to the event. Similarly, the report suggests the accessibility of supervisory support. It is likely that this would be provided in the form of regular individual or group debriefings. In this form of environment, a senior officer is also trained to identify officers who may be suffering adverse effects of frequent exposure to harrowing incidents.

Limitations to counselling skills

The limitations to counselling skills are clearly stipulated within the BAC code of conduct. Pivotal to their effectiveness is the professional's ability to recognize those individuals with whom the use of counselling skills may be contra-indicated. In the main, this is achieved through the professional's sensitivity towards behaviour which indicates that an individual is suffering from more deep seated problems. While the individual may not require immediate psychiatric admission, they may require professional support through their general practitioner (GP). With individuals suffering from clinical depression, panic attacks or delusions for example, the use of counselling skills can incur adverse reactions which neither the professional nor the individual themselves may be able to manage. Being sensitive to behaviours or histories which might indicate psychological difficulties requiring professional treatment enables the professional to take the appropriate action in accessing specialist treatment.

In the immediate aftermath of trauma, individuals whether professionals or victims of the event may need to contain their feelings, where not to do so would lead to them being overwhelmed. This may be driven by their responsibility for the well-being of others at the scene of the event or their knowledge that at that point their feelings would be overwhelming and undermine their ability to cope. In such instances it is important to avoid the use of counselling skills if in doing so this would reduce the individual's ability to control their feelings and behaviour. The following case illustrates this through the use of counselling skills employed by a non-professional unconsciously and with good intention:

> The fire officer carried the fourth of the burnt bodies of
> the young children from the house, still smouldering.
> They had died alone in the house. Their tiny bodies and
> faces were wracked in terror. Their mother, working a late
> shift, was yet to discover the loss of her whole family.
> He could visualize her now, the torturous guilt, the self-
> blame, the resounding loss and sense of responsibility
> which would haunt her throughout her life. Looking at
> the child, lost in thoughts, a hand was laid on his arm, a

well-meaning neighbour spoke softly, 'She was only 4'. The comment was incisive, breaking into his thoughts and thrusting the reality of the situation in among his own perceptions of the horror the mother was yet to experience. The touch, the soft voice, the interjection of reality together accessed the empathy and distress against which he had been defending himself.

This situation had stimulated the fire officer's own thoughts about the event. They may have been triggered by the event itself, the number of children involved, the circumstances under which they died, and so on. They may also have been compounded by factors relating to the officer's current circumstances, such as the ages of his own children (see Chapter 4 for further discussion of vulnerability and recovery factors in post traumatic stress). However, traumatic events are by their nature deeply disturbing and the associated feelings can be overwhelming. In the immediate aftermath, professionals may protect themselves from the reality of the situation by focusing on their specific role and avoiding an appreciation of their feelings which would otherwise interfere with their functioning effectively. To access underlying feelings at such times through the use of counselling skills is counter productive, intrusive and potentially damaging, in interfering with the professional's sense of control, maintenance of image and innate defences.

The value of counselling skills

Research has demonstrated that positive outcomes are achieved in the course of counselling in general, although these studies suffer from methodological problems inherent in conducting research under counselling conditions (see Luborsky 1993; Seligman 1995 for a fuller discussion). Further studies, although limited, have shown that paraprofessional helpers can be as effective as professional helpers, and in some cases even more helpful (Hattie *et al.* 1984). Equally, research has also highlighted the potential deleterious effects of the use of counselling in a professional capacity (see Mohr 1995). Criticism of counselling has also been levelled at the manipulative or malicious intent with which it can be used (Masson 1988; Eysenck 1994). Undoubtedly, counselling and counselling skills are powerful tools that can incur disturbing sequelae if used inappropriately. Yet this does not detract from the fact that if used proficiently by socially intelligent professionals, they can achieve positive outcomes for the professional and for the individual concerned.

The trained use of counselling skills can be an effective means of helping others, of facilitating the professional in their primary role, and increasing the professional's sense of competence and satisfaction on the job. Adverse effects can be avoided by training, supervision and sound awareness on the part of the professional of the limitations to the use of counselling skills. This involves an ability to recognize occasions on which to refrain from the use of counselling skills and, in the case of peers, to refer them to professional counselling. Individuals employing counselling skills need to

- appreciate the complexity of the helping process
- be familiar with positive and negative outcomes of using counselling skills
- appreciate that poor counselling skills can be harmful
- be aware that counselling skills can temporarily simulate feelings of intimacy
- comply with professional supervision and training requirements.

The cost of counselling skills

The use of counselling skills is an expensive proposition, both monetarily and psychologically. There are significant cost implications in trained professionals diverting their time and efforts to the active use of counselling skills whether in their role with the public or in their capacity as a peer supporter or supervisor. The time itself may be well justified if it achieves a successful outcome. The effective use of counselling skills must then be evaluated both from the outcomes they achieve and the time involved in achieving them. Research increasingly demonstrates that an effective outcome can be as efficiently achieved through focused and direct intervention (Quick 1996). The advent of result-oriented brief counselling, together with the financial dynamics of 'managed care', have led to the use of more direct and focused counselling skills.

Counselling skills are frequently effective through brief accurate interventions of a challenging or thought-provoking nature, which stimulate alternative modes of thinking about the problem or create insight in the individual to their assumptions about characteristic ways of behaving. An intelligent and insightful interpretation which accurately reflects the individual's dysfunctional perceptions can stay with the person in the years to come and provide an anchor against which to compare repetitions of the same behaviour. The following case illustrates the potential significance of a brief-focused intervention:

> In response to a disclosure of sexual harassment on a nurse by a member of his staff, the A and E registrar responded to the woman's concerns over the aftermath of the disclosure and its impact on all parties: 'You can't make things better for him. You don't need to make things alright for me.' In this intervention, the registrar had made explicit to the nurse that she did not need to assume control and management of the outcome of the situation. The negative sequelae of the perpetrator's actions were not the responsibility of the woman and were manageable for the registrar. This intervention highlighted the nurse's fundamental belief that she bore responsibility for creating order out of chaos.

The use of counselling skills in a focused, direct and time-conscious manner influences the public's expectations of the support proffered them. It serves to model interactions which are aimed at achieving a specific and effective outcome, allowing the individual to remain aware of the professional's primary objective. At the same time, it conveys the purposeful nature of the interaction and the boundaries to the encounter. The efficient and timely use of counselling skills, while enhancing the clarity and substance of the professional's relationship with the public, also has an impact ultimately on the perceived performance and productivity of the professional by the organization. In addition, the focused, time conscious use of counselling skills can assist in controlling sources of occupational stress such as overload, role conflict and role ambiguity.

The next chapter reviews the various components of counselling skills to determine what constitutes good practice in an emergency service setting.

Chapter 3

Counselling skills in action

Two young officers bolted up six flights of stairs in a dilapidated bed and breakfast. They were responding to an emergency call relating to a domestic dispute. Reaching the top landing they found two men, their faces inches apart, fists and bodies ready to fly into action. A woman with a distraught baby tucked under her arm was screaming abuse at one of the men. Through an open door, three small children sat amidst the deafening noise oblivious, locked into the fantasy unfolding on the TV. The officers, helmets removed, each began to talk to one of the two males, encroaching non-threateningly on their personal distance and increasing the space between the two. The incident ended with one officer downstairs reasoning with one of the men while the other restored the scene in the bed-sit to calm, at which point a formal warning was delivered to each and the dispute was resolved.

This incident was my first exposure as an occupational psychologist to working with the police. For the officers involved, this was a standard emergency call. The officers had conducted the incident with sychronized precision. It was a role they had played many times and were accomplished in. Their training in counselling skills had long since been assimilated into their general repertoire of behaviour, such that they were barely aware of the skills applied. Yet the sense of achievement in having controlled a potentially volatile situation successfully was evident. They had each maintained eye contact with the respective men, blocking the view of the other antagonist. This persistence served to gain the men's attention and begin to engage them in debate with the officers. Initially matching the men's raised voices, they lowered their voices, executing control through the speed and firmness of their pitch and tone. At the same time each moved slowly into the other's space, causing them to back away slightly, both removing them from the protagonist and asserting dominance. By the time the situation was under control and the men were calmer, a purposeful rapport had been created. The more volatile of the men had explained enough of his position to the officer to feel heard. Reluctantly he agreed to keep the peace, and the dispute was for the time being resolved.

Many components of counselling skills are evident in this encounter and were clearly applied to fulfil a primary goal of maintaining law and order. The use of counselling skills is an integral part of the emergency service professional's life, and fundamental to their fulfilling their primary task effectively and efficiently.

Basic counselling skills

Certain characteristics have been recognized as fundamental for the positive use of counselling skills. Congruence, empathy and regard, together with concreteness and immediacy, may be considered as core skills in establishing a rapport with an individual (Rogers 1980; Egan 1998). Examination of counselling skills in isolation can make them appear mechanical and purely functional. In practice they never emerge as such. Breaking them down serves to provide a template against which personal and professional effectiveness in the use of counselling skills can be retrospectively and internally evaluated and developed.

Congruence

Congruence refers to the authenticity of the communication between the professional and the individual (Egan 1998). It denotes the consistency between the professional's overt behaviour in their interaction with the individual and their covert feelings and thoughts. Essentially, it reflects the ability of the professional to act towards the other without pretence or simulated concern, to behave in a way which reflects their commitment and interest in the individual's welfare. The circumstances which the professional encounters may influence the extent to which they are able to express concern and genuineness while remaining congruent in their interaction. Verbalizing incongruent and un-comfortable feelings may be more effective in sustaining auth-entic interaction while, at the same time, the professional is able to model the safe communication of ambivalent feelings. Funda-mentally, the maintenance of congruence requires professionals to have resolved dilemmas in their own value system and their professional role (McLeod 1998). The struggle with congruence is illustrated in the following description by a young fire officer, attending one of his first road traffic incidents:

> Two old people were trapped in a car between two heavy goods vehicles. As we arrived, the car caught fire and the elderly couple burnt to death. We worked on releasing the driver of the other heavy goods vehicle, who had been clearly responsible for the collision. It was difficult assisting him during the recovery operation, while he persisted in complaining of the old people for their part in the collision. I felt angry towards him for their unnecessary death and his blaming of them. I found it difficult to appreciate the pain he must have been under, still trapped in his vehicle. I tried to relate to him professionally, but I know he could sense that I didn't want to be there and to assist him.

In this incident, the professional's presence was possibly counter-productive. The incongruency of the officer's non-verbal and verbal behaviours would have been evident to the driver and defeated the object of providing support to him.

Remaining congruent in this situation would involve pro-fessionals in being aware of their own ambivalence in rescuing the likely perpetrator of the event. Congruency may also be facilitated by the professionals drawing on an understanding of the function of denial in the face of overwhelming trauma, and knowing that any feelings of guilt or shame in the driver would be likely to be delayed. The driver's ability to recover psycholo-gically in the aftermath of the event would in itself be influenced by the ability of the professionals to act non-judgementally. If they were unable to act compassionately to him in the face of his errors, he would find it all the more difficult subsequently in coming to terms with the consequences of his actions. It is important for both the victims of the event and for the ongoing well-being of the professional that feelings of anger or injustice are expressed appropriately outside of the incident through debriefing, re-evaluation or reframing of their role.

Positive regard

Positive regard for others conveys a sense of respect and regard for the individual and for their life (Rogers 1967). It involves a non-judgemental perspective on the individual. This does not imply an acceptance of their values and behaviours. It does mean that their life is viewed with dignity and an understanding of the circumstances which may have contributed to their current life situation. The prefix 'unconditional' refers to the regard being proffered without its being reciprocated. This is particularly salient to emergency service work where the expression of positive regard may at times be tested to the limits. Emergency professionals are often confronted with verbal and physical abuse in response to their efforts to protect the lives of the public. In addition, the individuals with whom they are working may have endangered the lives of others, acted irresponsibly or with criminal intent. Positive regard is facilitated by a knowledge of the factors which contribute to offensive behaviour, and a commitment to control the offending behaviour in the interests of all involved.

Empathy

Empathy is the ability to perceive the world accurately as others see it, and to understand their reactions to their experiences (see Duan and Hill 1996 for a comprehensive overview). It entails an ability to communicate accurately that understanding to the other person. Hoffman (1987: 48) defines empathy as an 'affective response more appropriate to someone else's situation than to one's own'. Empathy denotes an inclination to be receptive to the individual's understanding of their world through the feelings and thoughts they communicate to us. It is underpinned by an ability to listen actively, attend and to refrain from judgement.

Empathic understanding is communicated through the professional intuitively feeding back to the individual their understanding of what the individual is feeling and thinking. This often
involves making explicit what is implied rather than directly
spoken. For instance, in the following example a newly promoted
senior nurse was speaking to a peer supporter outside of her
department:

> A senior nurse in accident and emergency complained of
> having to conceal her feelings from junior staff for fear
> of appearing foolish to them. She felt that they would
> think there was something lacking in her if she admitted
> feeling upset especially following bereavements. She went
> on to complain that there often wasn't anyone senior
> there at those times. 'You're supposed to control your
> feelings. The doctors just move on to the next case and
> leave us to manage the relatives and their distress'. The
> peer supporter, a paramedic, acknowledged the limits to
> his own 'being there', and reflected back to her her sense
> of isolation and desertion in her senior role. He also
> addressed the gender and role differences between them,
> through noting her feelings of being undervalued as a
> woman in a management position. He reaffirmed the
> stress she experienced in managing the care of the junior
> staff, the patients and their families. His personal
> experience of her role was limited to merely his interface
> with A and E but he was able to empathize with the
> feelings resulting from her work.

An ability to empathize is inherently limited by fundamental
differences in the individual experiences of others in terms of
religion, education, gender, culture and physiology. It can be
offensive to an individual to suggest that empathy can give the
professional an insight into the individual's particular life experience. Yet, on occasions, it can be an effective means of reducing
the diversity gap by developing an empathic, if limited, understanding, based on active attending and listening. Scott and
Borodovsky (1990) refer to empathic listening in this context as
'cultural role taking'. The effort involved in negotiating empathy
in itself creates a connection between the professional and the

individual and generates an environment of trust (Covey 1989). Ultimately, the achievement of a shared understanding of the individual's thoughts and feelings is paramount in the effective use of counselling skills.

These respective personal dispositions underpin the professional's effective use of counselling skills. These attributes are characteristic ways of behaving which can be trained and cultivated through self-awareness. This is usually an ongoing process in which interactions with individuals may frequently stimulate a re-evaluation of beliefs and values. The effective use of counselling skills is fundamentally a dynamic process, in which outcomes may be rewarding or may serve to disturb personal views of the world. Encounters may require the professional to question their ability to negotiate complex and demanding interactions which run counter to their personal objectives. Resolution of incongruencies in professional and personal worlds may never be complete but awareness of their existence can determine the appropriate actions to take. It is in this process that discussion with a designated supervisor can prove most useful (see Davis 1996 for a comprehensive discussion of empathy).

Concreteness

Concreteness refers to the professional's capacity to be clear and explicit in their interactions with an individual and to help the individual to express themselves clearly. This is fundamental to effective communication. Concreteness involves the professional worker helping the individual to make explicit the issues and concerns which are being inferred but may not be directly spoken. This encourages the individual to be specific and facilitates a greater understanding in the transaction. At the same time, it serves to generate a more transparent, open and direct communication process. For individuals who are unaccustomed to making explicit their needs and having them openly acknowledged, this in itself can be an informative and supportive experience.

A fire officer attended a fire in an elderly man's home. Once the fire was under control, the man complained of pains in his right arm. He was clearly distracted and concerned about the pain, yet continued to refuse further assistance. The officer suggested to the man that he might be afraid the pain was associated with his heart and that it might be serious. The man continued to deny any such fears. The professional suggested that he might be concerned about what might happen to his house if he went to hospital. He then began to talk about the strangers in his house bothering him, and now having no working lock on the door, and having to restore his home. The professional was able to make explicit the man's confusion, making sense of his ambiguous communication, through the use of questions and empathy, and reflecting it back to the man in a concrete manner.

Immediacy

Immediacy entails an intention to focus clearly on the immediate issue which has brought the professional into play. It requires a focused application of skills to address the current situation and the immediate problems which it generates (Carkhuff 1987). Any immediate problem is commonly founded on preceding difficulties which may have contributed to it. This may stimulate the individual to reprocess underlying concerns and thoughts. To recall previous disturbing events may be counter-productive in compounding the individual's current distress. Focusing directly on recovery of the immediate situation may also be effective in promoting a sense of control and mastery of the event, and contribute to the development of effective coping strategies. It may also require the professional to address any issues, such as diversity, which interfere with fulfilling their role.

Challenging

Challenging dysfunctional mind sets and perspectives of individuals may be necessary in an effort to engage behaviour appropriate to the circumstances. An individual's thoughts and feelings and views of the world often determine the way in which they behave. These views may be misinformed, inaccurate and self-defeating. Challenging self-limiting thought processes may enable the individual to consider more effective problem-managing action. This may take the form of introducing alternative ways of thinking about a problem or developing insight in the individual into the ways in which they may be contributing to the problems they encounter. This can encourage the individual to assume responsibility for their problems. It may also serve to increase their awareness of the control they are able to exercise over their circumstances to bring about changes.

In many instances, dysfunctional views can be self-serving and allow the individual to rationalize their current life circumstances or their lack of appropriate action (see Halleck 1988; Snyder and Higgins 1988 for a fuller discussion of excuse-making behaviour). Individuals also instinctively defend their perceptions and beliefs. Modelling interpersonal skills may enable them to be more receptive to the views of others and more willing to adjust their attitudes to accommodate those of others.

> The paramedics had been called to a domestic incident
> in which a woman had been reportedly injured. They
> arrived at the house to find the woman distressed and
> with a minor injury to her arm. They were further faced
> with a family dispute between a father and his son. The
> father was threatening his son and struggling with his
> feelings of rage. The situation was rapidly escalating
> towards a violent confrontation between the two of them
> while the woman tried to prevent this with an equal
> distribution of verbal abuse to all parties. Having diffused
> the emotional level of the confrontational behaviour, and
> controlled the immediate scene, the officers were able to
> briefly model listening and acknowledging skills, making
> explicit the differences in the views between the parties
> and encouraging empathy. They were also in a position
> to challenge the father's declarations that his son was
> lazy and would never make anything, making explicit
> his own responsibility and contribution to his son's
> self-beliefs.

Interventions of this kind are limited by their nature and may be short lived, which can add to their feeling of futility. It is likely

that such scenarios will be re-enacted and may continue to require the intervention of the emergency services in some form
or other. Yet the introduction of different perspectives and a
challenging of rigid attitudes, together with the modelling of
alternative behaviours, can begin to raise doubts and shift perceptions in some cases. Frequently, a brief and apt comment from
a professional, with the intrinsic authority their role carries,
may well remain with an individual and lead to a change in an
otherwise ingrained self-perception.

Self-disclosure

Self-disclosure on the part of the professional can be helpful in
forming a more immediate rapport with the individual (Edwards
and Murdock 1994). It can serve to reduce some of the inherent
tension in the situation by which an individual is thrust into
a sensitive situation with a stranger. For the professional to
self-disclose may make the interaction more equal, and reduce
potential barriers to communication. It may also model for the
individual appropriate disclosure. It is important that professionals remain sensitive to the individual's reactions to their disclosure of feelings or thoughts relating to themselves.

It can be counter-productive if it raises the individual's
awareness of the extent of any differences between the two of
them, culturally, socially or educationally for example. It may
also have the adverse effect of increasing the intimacy of the
situation beyond that which the individual can manage. Self-
disclosure, in addition to the authority inherent in the professional's role, can simulate a powerful sense of intimacy (Goodyear
and Shumate 1996). It is important that any self-disclosure is
communicated clearly in the context of the individual's professional role to avoid it being misconstrued.

Self-disclosure should be appropriate to the situation and
limited in its content and frequency. It should be selective and
focused with the clear intention of achieving the purpose of
making the situation more manageable to the individual, or to
enable the individual to cooperate more easily with professionals
in their primary role. Any disclosure should not be burdensome
to the individual, nor of a nature that will remain with the

individual long after the event (see Weiner 1983 for an extensive discussion of this skill).

Attending

Attending is the function of focusing alert attention on the individual. It is a matter of applying all senses actively to the individual in an effort to understand their feelings and their experience of their situation. Attending is expressed through physical, non-verbal behaviours such as eye contact, physical posture and proximity. The professional's non-verbal behaviour such as voice tone, strength and speed of speech can be instrumental in conveying to the individual a sense of control over the situation and engendering a calmness or cooperativeness in them, depending on the circumstances (Knapp 1978). Similarly, the use of nods and minimal prompts such as 'yes', 'no' or 'mm' may indicate the professional's understanding of what the individual is saying.

Stance should portray an open posture and an availability to the communications of the other, such as facing the individual without crossed limbs or glazed expression. The adoption of a relaxed posture on the part of the professional can be effective in enabling the individual to relax. Mirroring postures, such as leaning towards the individual while not invading their personal space, can communicate an attentiveness to the other. The conscious application of attention should be informed by cultural and gender differences (Sue 1990). Prolonged eye contact in certain cultures can be interpreted as aggressive or unnatural. Similarly, physical proximity can be experienced as inappropriate or uncomfortable according to gender or age.

Professionals can also derive further insight into the state of the individual by attending to their personal physical and emotional reactions to the other. Feelings of physical tension, emotional mood and intuition can be indicative of covert communications from the individual which would not otherwise be made explicit (see Hill *et al.* 1993 for a discussion of 'covert processes').

The emergency nurse felt physically tense and somewhat sad as the old woman spoke to him and pleasantly thanked him for his help following her fall. She had been satisfactorily treated and was now ready to be discharged. Pursuing his feelings, he probed further about her professed feelings of liking the home in which she lived. In affording her the time to listen and attend, he gained her trust and through that learned that her fall was not accidental. In her fear of remaining in residential care where she felt intimidated, she had resorted to self-harm in an effort to gain access to long-term hospital care. This information later allowed the underlying and contributory problems to be confronted, which could otherwise have led to an unnecessary replication of the incident.

Listening

Listening involves three components: understanding the individual's verbal communications; observing their non-verbal behaviours such as posture, facial expressions, tone of voice; and placing their communications in the context of their current circumstances. Facial expressions and tone of voice can be a more accurate reflection of the individual's state of mind than what they say. Where inconsistencies exist between non-verbal communication and the spoken word, it is more likely that non-verbal behaviour is more reliable (Ekman 1992). Listening to each of these sources of communication can allow the professional to adjust and moderate the use of counselling skills accordingly (Nelson-Jones 1996).

The individual's spoken communications are about feelings, thoughts and events as they happened. Depending on the role of the emergency service professional, the significance of these components differs in importance. The active use of counselling skills by the professional will be directed towards gathering the specific information which will inform the professional's actions and allow them to fulfil their primary role. For instance, a paramedic will focus the individual's attention on the physical site of pain and discomfort and will seek information which may give an indication of the nature of the injury incurred. A fire officer may need to ascertain information immediately pertaining to the imminent danger to which the individual and others may be exposed. The goal will be to make the scene safe prior to being able to take further action, and so engage the individual's cooperation to this effect.

Active interventions

Active interventions on the part of the professional may involve the use of questions, clarification and the active development of empathy. The use of these interventions is influenced by the professional's objectives in the specific situation which is encountered. Counselling skills may then be applied as appropriate. These may fulfil a variety of functions such as the diffusion of emotional tension in conflict or crisis situations, the clarification of information on which the professional must act or the cooperation of the individual in their own recovery or rescue. Any use of interventions should avoid the professional projecting their perceptions or values on to the individual.

Questions

Questions can form an effective component of counselling skills (Hough 1998). Open questions can serve to elicit more information by allowing the client to expand on their understanding of the event, and to facilitate exploration of their understanding of the situation. It can lead to a clarification of understanding in the perception of both the individual and the professional where the situation is fundamentally ambiguous. At the same time, this may also allow the professional to focus on the non-verbal communications and to avoid following unconfirmed assumptions.

The use of closed questions can serve to focus the individual's attention and direct the communication in a positive and determined manner. Their use in this way serves to funnel the questions towards a preconceived area of focus which may be important in proffering appropriate support to the individual at times of crisis. The professional may pre-empt the use of closed questions by communicating to the individual the purpose of the questions and allow the individual to cooperate consciously or to decline from responding. The use of closed questions should be tempered by an awareness of appropriate boundaries. This is particularly important in situations of crisis which by their nature may have compromised normal boundaries.

Reflection

Reflection is the process of repeating the last phrase that the individual used in order to encourage the person to say more. Echoing the individual's last thought stimulates them to continue talking in an effort to clarify their words and relate their feelings more clearly to the professional (Nelson-Jones 2000). Reflections of this kind usually mirror the individual's tone of voice to avoid being mistaken as a question or disturbing the individual's line of thought. Used unobtrusively, reflections can be useful interventions, particularly where the individual needs to be distracted from pain or activity surrounding them in the event of a crisis situation. Selectively reflecting back certain aspects of the individual's conversation can also direct the focus of the communication towards a specific topic which may be central to the professional's primary role.

> The paramedic, having stabilized the condition of the driver of the car, sat with him continuing to monitor him as the fire service fought to release him. The driver, while in considerable pain, was worrying about his survival; and if he died, who would then look after his children. In an effort to distract him from the pain and the surrounding noise, the paramedic drew him to talk about his children, who had lost their mother some time ago following a long terminal illness. Amidst his pain, his thoughts were wandering and unfocused, but the paramedic sustained his preoccupations with his children by reflecting back his end phrases. In doing this, the driver became absorbed in his feelings for his children and his intention to survive. Specific questions would have disturbed his line of thought. Through the use of reflection and intermittent open questions, the paramedic was able to help the driver to control his feelings of pain and panic and gain his cooperation in remaining calm during the rescue operation.

Confrontation

Confrontation is a counselling skill frequently employed by emergency service professionals in the event of death, injury, fire or criminal activity. It may also be required in the course of interaction in the following circumstances (Egan 1998):

- compulsive, negative self-statements, such as 'I'll never recover'
- manipulative behaviour or self-deceptive behaviour
- clarification of an issue which requires direct action
- making explicit covert or incongruent communications
- challenging behaviours such as complacency, procrastination, denying or avoiding responsibility.

Informing individuals of disturbing or unpalatable information involves anticipating the individual's fear, distress and anger and feeling confident in being able to manage those feelings. This entails professionals being aware of their own reactions to the expression of strong feelings. Anticipation of disclosing horrific or negative news to another can naturally evoke physiological and emotional reactions in the professional which are mutually unhelpful. These natural fears and anxieties may be diminished by repeated exposure to the event, working as a team to manage the incident effectively, debriefing and focusing attention on the positive effects of the professional's contribution. The following description by a police officer demonstrates the resounding impact of bereavement on all involved:

> I was called to an accident at a house. The father had been building on to the lounge. He'd put a door across the access to stop his toddler getting in, and blocked the door with a bucket of broken glass. The toddler had scrambled over the door and fallen into the bucket. A piece of glass had pierced him through the heart. I waited alone at the scene for the father to return to break the news to him. I sat with him through his anguished cries, his distress, anger towards himself and unbearable guilt. I can still hear and see the scene today.

This incident demonstrates the magnitude of the father's suffering and the apparent limitations at the time of any use of counselling skills. Yet, in this example, the police officer, in having broken the news to the father appropriately, provided a safe and containing environment for the father's anger and distress. The officer remained with the father and would have been able to have challenged his assumptions about his guilt and feelings of personal responsibility. Being alone in breaking the news reduced the necessity for other strangers and softened the official nature of the event. However, this also imposed more pressure on the officer during the delay in the father's return. It is important that in events of this kind, professionals receive debriefing, both to avoid their own vicarious traumatization and to allow their efforts after such a devastating event to be viewed positively.

Summary

Training in the use of counselling skills can improve communication, clarify understanding, challenge dysfunctional perceptions and promote empathy and emotional support in crises. These skills enable professionals to achieve their primary goals and, in so doing, can also increase personal job satisfaction and commitment. Nevertheless, the efforts involved in the constant and focused use of counselling skills mainly in interaction with strangers can deplete the professional's resources. To sustain this level of interaction requires not only formal supervision and debriefing but also the support of a working culture which extends the same intrinsic values of listening, attending, empathy and respect to those who operate within it.

Fundamental to the effective use of counselling skills within the emergency service environment is a knowledge of the psychological effects of traumatic incidents. The next chapter discusses the signs and symptoms of post traumatic stress and suggests supportive means of intervention.

Further reading

Bor, R., Miller, R., Latz, M. and Sait, H. (1998) *Counselling in Health Care Settings*. London: Massell.

Davis, M.H. (1994) *Empathy: A Social Psychological Approach*. Oxford: Westview Press.

Egan, G. (1998) *The Skilled Helper: A Problem-Management Approach to Helping*, 6th edn. Pacific Grove, CA: Brooks/Cole.

Hough, M. (1998) *Counselling Skills and Theory*. London: Hodder and Stoughton.

Jacobs, M. (1998) *The Presenting Past: The Core of Psychodynamic Counselling and Therapy*, 2nd edn. Buckingham: Open University Press.

McLeod, J. (1998) *An Introduction to Counselling*, 2nd edn. Buckingham: Open University Press.

Meier, S.T. and Davis, S.R. (1997) *The Elements of Counseling*. Pacific Grove, CA: Brooks/Cole.

Nelson-Jones, R. (2000) *Introduction to Counselling Skills*. London: Sage.

Woolfe, R. and Dryden, W. (eds) (1996) *Handbook of Counselling Psychology*. London: Sage.

Chapter **4**

Working with post traumatic stress

Emergency service personnel predominantly work with individuals involved in traumatic events. Although most people exposed to trauma will recover from their experiences to function as normal, they are still likely to undergo the characteristic symptoms of post traumatic stress disorder (PTSD).

Post traumatic stress disorder

PTSD is potentially stimulated by any experience that exposes the individual to a traumatic event in which there is a threat of death or serious injury to the individual or to others (DSM IV: American Psychiatric Association (APA) 1994). As a result of this exposure, the individual experiences a specific set of physiological and psychological responses to the traumatic incident. These reactions include intrusive thoughts and images of the incident, a sense of numbness to events, hyperalertness, or avoidance of reminders of the event (see Table 4.1). Any one or a combination of these events may have a marked effect on the individual's normal psychosocial functioning.

'Intrusion' or involuntary reprocessing of the traumatic memories following the incident is a deeply disturbing experience which may take the form of constant rumination, flashbacks or nightmares. However, this process in the first instance can

Table 4.1   DSM IV criteria for post traumatic stress disorder

A	The individual experienced or witnessed a traumatic event that involved actual or threatened death or serious injury to themselves or others, which caused them intense fear, helplessness or horror.
B	The distressing event is persistently re-experienced in the form of intrusive, disturbing thoughts, images or dreams of the event. The individual may experience intense psychological distress on exposure to events symbolic of the traumatic experience/s. They may also experience sensations of the event recurring (flashbacks) and/or feelings of guilt associated with behaviour at the time of the event.
C	Persistent avoidance of thoughts, feelings, activities or situations reminiscent of the event or numbing of responsiveness to others, and to activities. The individual may also experience an inability to feel warmth toward others, an inability to recall aspects of the event, and a sense of foreshortened future.
D	Persistent symptoms of increased arousal. This may take the form of physiologic reactivity at exposure to events that are reminiscent of an aspect of the event, difficulty concentrating or sleeping, irritability, hyper-vigilance or increased startle response.
E	Duration of the disturbance of at least one month. Symptoms may not be immediately evident but may be exhibited some time after the event. In this instance they would be classified as delayed.
F	The disturbance incurs clinical distress or impairment of normal social or workplace functioning.
	Acute: duration of symptoms less than three months *Chronic:* symptoms persist beyond three months *Delayed:* symptoms emerge at least six months after the trauma

Source: American Psychiatric Association 1994

serve the purpose of modifying the feelings associated with the trauma and can foster a tolerance for the disturbing content of the recollections (Horowitz 1978). Avoidance of situations, thoughts or feelings symbolic of the event can be equally immobilizing, preventing the individual from fully processing the disturbing thoughts and feelings. While initially this may serve the purpose of protecting the individual from the overwhelming nature of the event, in the long term this will be counter-productive to the individual's recovery.

Persistent symptoms of increased arousal will interfere with the individual's sleeping pattern, preventing them from falling asleep or causing them to wake in the early hours in a state of high alertness. The individual will be more likely to react irritably and have great difficulty concentrating or settling on one activity for long. They will also be hyper-vigilant of their environment, monitoring it closely, startling easily and primed for action. Hyper-arousal is strongly associated with intrusive imagery and thoughts of the traumatic event.

Most people who experience traumatic stress reactions will recover within a period of four weeks. However, some people are unable to integrate their experiences over time and the characteristic reactions of intrusion, avoidance and hyper-arousal associated with PTSD fail to abate. These symptoms may then interfere with the individual's normal everyday functioning. To constitute a diagnosis of PTSD, the symptoms must have persisted beyond four weeks and not have been present prior to the traumatic incident. However, PTSD may also be delayed and symptoms emerge some time after the event either as a result of a subsequent trauma or spontaneously (see van der Kolk *et al.* 1996 for further discussion of PTSD symptomology).

Secondary symptoms

In addition to the listed DSM IV diagnostic criteria, a number of further symptoms have been noted in individuals manifesting classic PTSD (see Appendix A). These are classed as 'Associated Features' in DSM IV (APA 1994: 424) and include reactions such as *'survivor guilt'* in which the individual experiences disturbing self-recriminations in relation to their survival often at the expense of others. This overriding feeling of guilt may be evident in the immediate aftermath of the event. Other symptoms may emerge at different stages and often serve to mask the predominant features of PTSD. These include depression, anxiety, substance abuse, chronic exhaustion and significant deterioration in work performance. These additional symptoms are important in the recognition and understanding of traumatic stress behaviour both at home and in the workplace.

Crisis interventions

PTSD, if chronic or delayed in onset, is much more difficult to treat. It is currently believed that early intervention in traumatic events facilitates emotional processing, although research as yet is sparse (Joseph *et al.* 1997). Stein (1977) proposed a model of crisis intervention counselling which includes on-the-scene support with follow-up within two days. For the majority of individuals involved in smaller scale traumatic incidents, further counselling may not be readily available. However, emergency professionals may be able to provide details on referral resources, and identify those individuals who are likely to require specialist intervention and encourage them to access it. Confidential debriefings held within two to three days of the trauma are generally found to promote recovery. Any sooner and the individuals are too disorientated and preoccupied for them to be of value. Interventions by emergency personnel in the immediate aftermath can be instrumental in initiating effective coping measures. The support provided by the emergency professional together with information on responses to traumatic events and their normality can be pivotal to the individual's continuing recovery (see Yule 1999 for further discussion of the development of PTSD).

Immediate aftermath of the trauma

Emergency service professionals, in the main, are dealing with individuals immediately following a traumatic event, when the potential for interventions aimed at recovery will be minimal. The professional's primary role is of orientation of the individual, demonstrating control in the midst of the chaos, providing safety and containment, and remaining empathic to the individual's feelings. The emergency professional's interactions with the traumatized individual at this time, although seemingly limited, is likely to stay in the individual's memory in association with the traumatic incident and may ultimately assist their recovery.

Practical help

The significance of practical help in the immediate aftermath of the event cannot be underestimated. People may be unaware of the full extent of the incident, including their own or others' injuries, and may be concerned about immediate responsibilities. Providing information on the incident and on significant others who may have been involved in it will allay unnecessary fears. In addition, solving practical problems, such as children to be collected, will be of considerable help to the survivor. Referring to larger scale traumatic incidents, Joseph *et al.* (1997: 112) write: 'Individuals who are in shock may need quiet to rest and protection from the most intrusive agents of the media'. In providing such assistance, the professional is demonstrating a control over the event and its aftermath and bringing order into an otherwise alarmingly chaotic experience for the individual.

Physiological reactions

In the immediate aftermath of a traumatic event, people are in a state of physical shock. The physiological reactions they experience are alarming to them and heighten their sense of loss of control and helplessness. Symptoms such as *hyper-arousal*, rapid heart rate, nausea and difficulties in breathing reinforce their sense of fear, panic and hyper-alertness. Many survivors of trauma report *time distortions* in which the traumatic incident appeared to happen in slow motion. In addition, people might report *tunnel vision* in which they saw only the traumatic event itself and all peripheral images appeared blurred. The combination of the event itself and the physiological symptoms they experience create for the individual an overwhelming psychological experience. A consciousness of their own disturbing reactions to the event and the unexpectedness of them heightens their sense of fear and possibly of shame. For the professional to demonstrate an understanding of the symptoms that the survivor is experiencing tempers any feelings of 'madness' the individual might be feeling and promote a sense of relatedness. The sound of a voice and particularly its tone can provide an anchor for the individual to the present and create a sense of calm and control over the situation.

Intrusion and dissociation

People may experience characteristic reactions of PTSD such as intrusion, in which they are preoccupied with the traumatic event and recycle the images of it in their mind. They may attempt to make sense of what happened, focusing on the fine details of the event, wanting to know the causal effects. They may switch between the 'here and now' and the events surrounding the incident. Their thought pattern may appear erratic and incoherent and interspersed with overwhelming distress or anger. Conversely, they may, in their preoccupation, appear dissociated, that is, inert and removed from the events happening around them. Dissociation can serve the purpose of affording the survivor some protection from pain, anguish and disturbing feelings. However, maintaining communication with the individual, using appropriate physical contact and consciously interrupting the individual's thoughts can draw them back to the 'here and now' and prevent them recycling the memory of the trauma and reinforcing it. In a situation in which the individual has no control, is helpless and in overwhelming pain, the professional can still communicate a sense of being there and a control over the situation.

> I hadn't been in the job long. One night we were called out to a disused industrial site. A building had partially collapsed. A youth, still conscious, was trapped in there below an iron girder. He was calling out to his mates in fear and pain. He fell quiet and didn't speak again. I talked to him while we worked to get him out. I didn't think he would survive. Afterwards, he said me talking had helped him cut out the rest. He couldn't remember much else of the rescue operation other than that.

This scene illustrates how maintaining an interaction with the survivor can enable him, to some extent, to escape the horror of the scene of which he is a part. Maintaining a relatedness, regardless of the responsiveness of the individual at the time, can have a delayed effect on outcome. Thus enabling the individual to recall the presence of others at the scene and their support in the midst of the horror of the event. The rescue often forms a central focus of the traumatic experience and the disturbing recollection of it may be moderated in part by the interventions of emergency service professionals.

Amnesia and avoidance

People may be unable to remember events leading up to the trauma. Similarly, in the aftermath of the event they may also find themselves unable to recall personal details of a general nature. At this time, professionals can be instrumental in reassuring them that this is a normal reaction to an abnormal event and reducing the pressure on them to remember. At this stage it is also common for individuals to demonstrate avoidance of thoughts or feelings reminiscent of the trauma. While this may be necessary for the individual to cope in the immediate aftermath, if it persists it will be counter-productive in the long term to recovery. Under these circumstances it would be beneficial for the survivor to be referred on to a counsellor, and assisted in overcoming resistance to do so (Scott and Palmer 2000 give an overview of professional therapies).

Fear and anguish

The event may also stimulate fears in the individual, whether realistic or not, for the safety of other family members. Trauma has the immediate effect of shattering an individual's sense of invulnerability, and stimulates a heightened sense of impending danger. This may result in individuals experiencing undue concern for the welfare of family members, their safety or the impact of the trauma on them. For the professional to acknowledge the individual's fears and reframe their concerns may help diffuse any unnecessary anxiety. However, if family members are involved in the incident, their fears may be well founded and it may not be possible to give assurance. Individuals may see family members who are dead, mutilated or seriously injured. In such circumstances, providing a safe and containing environment for them to express their feelings, while essential, can be a demanding task. It is in these situations in which despair and anguish predominate, and there is least opportunity for constructive action, that professionals can benefit from mandatory debriefing to protect their own well-being.

> Attended RTA [road traffic accident] with the Hospital Flying Squad. Five youths in one car all died. Three

bodies lay beside the car covered with blankets, just a row of jeans and sneakers showing. One boy was resting against his friend, who later died in theatre. A passer-by sat behind the boy consoling him and holding him while we worked in vain to save him. (She was so helpful and I wondered later if she had received any help.) The mother arrived at the scene, hysterical. There was nothing we could do to save her this sight. Five young bodies lying there side by side in the road, one her son, with all the noise and activity surrounding them. Her screams against their silence. I felt so helpless.

This scene illustrates the tension for emergency personnel when it seems as if there can be no constructive action, nothing at all to be done. Yet being with the individual in the depth of their despair, containing their anguish, is what is most needed. While there is no protection from the horror of the event, the presence and support of trained professionals can make a difference. In this vignette, the nurse is highly conscious of the young life they failed to save and is faced with the reality, which in part drives her, the mother's loss of her child, with four similar tragedies yet to unfold. The lack of successful outcome for the nurse may reduce her resilience to the trauma, and affect her ability to intervene effectively with the mother. Knowing that this is when support skills are most needed yet when they may appear least effective is important to the professional who can otherwise be immobilized by a sense of personal failure.

Viewing the body

Surviving family members may wish to view the body of the person who died even if disfigured or if any deterioration has occurred. In most instances this has been found to be helpful, with the exception of instances in which there has been a delay in the recovery of the body and decomposure is advanced (Joseph *et al.* 1997). Hodgkinson *et al.* (1993), referring to larger scale trauma, suggest that the bereaved should not be encouraged to view but, should they wish to do so, they should not be deterred. Equally, bereaved relatives should be offered access to any documentation pertaining to the inquest, which may involve photographs of the body. The emergency professional can be supportive at this stage by ensuring that the bereaved understand the formal proceedings and are allowed to exercise some control and choice over the process. Access to emotional support from significant others, and an environment in which the individual is able to express feelings, will be tantamount to their well-being. Again, the professional may be in a position to promote these conditions.

Trauma membrane

Some individuals may also be clearly disturbed by the trauma yet not react openly. This is often evident in those who help others at the scene of an incident in either a professional capacity or as family members. Their resources are directed into coping with the immediate event and those more heavily involved in it. This can be a necessary coping strategy and is often referred to as a trauma membrane. It is important that these natural defences are not broken and that there is a level of collusion in enabling the individual to avoid overwhelming feelings which would prevent them from otherwise managing the situation. In this situation, it would be inappropriate to access feelings at all. Offering indirect support by being present and being available is often most appreciated. For individuals to believe that they are able to make a difference at the scene and positively affect the outcome of the event will ultimately support their recovery. The following illustration demonstrates the power of an inappropriate reaction on the ability of the individual to cope with the situation in a way he would have chosen.

> The man was knelt beside his teenage daughter, still trapped in the car. As he talked to her, she was drifting in and out of consciousness. When the fire crew arrived to cut her out, he was clearly disturbed. He stood back from the car, attempting to distract himself, from his feelings, from the reality of it all. He called out to one of the crew for more information. One of the witnesses from another vehicle approached him, and put her arm on his,

offering comfort. He reacted immediately in anger and then distress. Overwhelmed, he struggled with his feelings, returning to be with his daughter amidst the wreckage. Now overcome, he couldn't help his daughter as he wanted to, and like we would have wanted.

Normalizing reactions

The professional can play a significant role in normalizing the individual's reactions and feelings and forewarning them or their family members of the symptoms they may experience following the trauma. Providing information on the effects of PTSD is a primary intervention which is required in most traumatic incidents at some stage and will be important to the individual's long term recovery. For individuals returning home, it is important for their own safety that they are not left alone at a time when they are still likely to be preoccupied with the traumatic incident. Traumatized survivors find considerable difficulty in concentrating and focusing on activities in the here and now, rendering them more susceptible to accidents.

Social support

Access to sustained assurance and support after the trauma can often significantly aid the survivor's recovery. The emergency professional can be instrumental in promoting the individual's use of social support in the immediate aftermath of the traumatic incident. In the first instance, emotional support is more effective. Empathic listening as a form of emotional support can be therapeutic to individuals, during the period in which they are experiencing intrusive imagery and are compelled to talk about their experiences in an effort to process them. However, while the person is driven to recycle thoughts about the event, doing so repeatedly can serve to reinforce the compulsive re-processing. It is important that the individual is encouraged to engage in other activities. Introducing new experiences in this way can help the survivor to blend new and recent memories with the traumatic ones. In the days following the traumatic incident, cognitive support becomes more effective, by which the person can be assisted in attributing meaning to the event and reframing inappropriate attributions of blame or guilt.

Period following the trauma

Debriefing

While further interventions in the immediate aftermath are limited, formal debriefings, within a period of 24–72 hours, conducted by trained mental health professionals can be beneficial to subsequent recovery. Formal debriefings consist of a structured process in which individuals will recall the facts of the event, express their thoughts in response to it, their reactions to it, and be informed of the symptoms to expect. Group debriefings can provide a medium to share perceptions of the event, to learn more of the normality of post traumatic stress and to mobilize mutual support (Dyregrov 1989).

Intrusion

Within the next few days after the traumatic event, emergency professionals who are dealing with traumatized individuals are likely to find them preoccupied with the trauma, driven to recount the event, concerned with missing details, explanations and meanings. They may want to piece the event together and to make sense of the causal factors to achieve a more complete understanding of the course of events leading to the trauma. Providing them with the opportunity to talk about the trauma, reframing distorted perceptions of it such as attribution of blame and residual feelings of guilt or shame will help the person. Such interventions may need frequent reinforcement for the individual to be able to internalize an alternative interpretation of their role in the trauma. It is important as people 'relive' traumatic events to interrupt their recall of the event intermittently to avoid retraumatization by the memory. This also serves the purpose of overlaying the trauma memory with recollections of the professional's interruptions.

A baby 3 months old, one of twins born at 32 weeks. He had suffered respiratory arrest. All attempts to revive him failed. Watching the attempts to revive him, then being with the father as he cuddled and talked to the baby, was heartbreaking. He repeated over to the baby how he had felt and what had happened since the baby's birth. Each time he went over it he remembered more details. I said things too about the baby, even though he didn't seem to hear. I knew that if I started to cry I wouldn't be able to stop. After the shift, half way down the road I burst into tears. I cried all the way home. My husband is very supportive in those situations.

In this illustration, the father demonstrates his preoccupation with the trauma. He had probably already played over in his mind much of the trauma as it had unfolded for him since the baby's birth. Now that his worst fear had happened, he needed to talk. The gentle interruptions in his recollections and the presence of someone who was not detached from his suffering would become a positive aspect of this part of the trauma memory. In addition, this vignette also demonstrates the nurse's efforts to apply herself to the event in order to cope and to feel effective she struggles to contain her own feelings until she is in a safe and, to her, appropriate place.

Hyper-arousal

People who are traumatized behave differently. They more readily suffer from hyper-arousal and have more difficulty in self-calming. The physiological arousal they experience overrides any cognitive rationale they may have of the event. For example, if a person who has experienced physical attacks is faced with the sudden and rapid movement of another towards them, they may react in fear. Once having identified that the gesture was in fact one of affection, physiologically they may well continue to react as if under attack. Reacting to such 'triggers' in this way can be disconcerting in recognizing the inappropriateness of their reaction and yet being unable to control it. Similarly, following traumatic experiences, people may startle more easily in response to sudden actions or loud noises. This raised level of arousal will feel physically uncomfortable to the individual, and will usually be accompanied by a general irritability. It is helpful if the professional creates, through their voice and behaviour, a sense of calmness. Equally for the person to be physically active at such times will allow them to expend some of the energy, dissipating the adrenalin (see van der Kolk *et al.* 1996 for physiological changes resulting from early or prolonged exposure to trauma).

Avoidance

In the days following the trauma, individuals who appear to be affected by the traumatic incident, and yet are avoiding thoughts or feelings associated with the event, may well develop prolonged post traumatic stress reactions. Their avoidance may be necessary, founded on the need for stronger defences against the emotional impact of the event, possibly due to underlying traumatic experiences or personality dispositions. In such instances, it is important that the individual is referred on to a mental health professional for individual trauma counselling (Follette *et al.* 1998 give an overview of treatment interventions). However, not all individuals who appear unpossessed by the trauma are necessarily avoiding or denying the impact. It is frequently the case that people involved in traumatic incidents do not experience symptoms of post traumatic stress. Some survivors undergo horrific traumatic events and experience no adverse effects at all. There may be many reasons for this, such as personality, simulated or actual experiences of incidents, the cognitive appraisal of the event, or the extent of the individual's contribution to the success of the outcome of the event. In such cases, it must be stressed to the individual that while PTSD is a normal reaction to an abnormal event, not everyone experiences it, and it is not abnormal not to do so.

Positive outcomes

Much of the literature on exposure to traumatic events emphasizes the severity and chronicity of traumatic events. Yet traumatic events can often incur positive reactions such as a re-evaluation of life, and an increased compassion for others (Joseph *et al*. 1993). It is argued that among those individuals exposed to large scale disasters who do not exhibit adverse reactions to their experience, there is often a major attitudinal change in their outlook on life as a direct result of their traumatic experience. Further research into such responses may be of value in the development of proactive interventions.

Most people involved in traumatic incidents experience symptoms characteristic of PTSD. These symptoms in themselves are disturbing in their unexpectedness. Emergency professionals are in a position to be instrumental in assisting survivors in coping with the horror of their experience, initially by communicating an understanding of how the person feels through the use of basic counselling skills, but also, by normalizing the person's reactions and raising their or their family's awareness of the symptoms they may experience in the aftermath of the event. In the few days following the event, the professional may employ cognitive support, that is allowing the person to talk about their experiences in an effort to process them. At this stage, formal debriefing or trauma counselling by mental health professionals can be most effective. Informing people of the resources available to them, and identifying those who would benefit from specialist intervention, can be of help to individuals or family members who might not be familiar with the benefits of counselling.

For emergency personnel, regularly managing both the traumatic event and the psychological and emotional reactions of traumatized people can be a demanding and disturbing feature of the job, rendering them susceptible to vicarious traumatization. The next chapter examines the particular sources and signs of traumatic stress on emergency professionals.

Further reading

Figley, C. (ed.) (1994) *Trauma and its Wake*. New York: Brunner Mazel.
Herman, J.L. (1992) *Trauma and Recovery: From Domestic Abuses to Political Terror*. London: HarperCollins.

Mitchell, J. and Bray, G. (1990) *Emergency Services Stress: Guidelines for Preserving the Health and Careers of Emergency Service Personnel.* Englewood Cliffs, NJ: Prentice Hall.

Scott, M.J. and Palmer, S. (2000) *Trauma and Post Traumatic Stress Disorder.* London: Cassell.

Soloman, S.D., Wilson, J. and Keane, T.M. (1997) *Assessing Psychological Trauma and PTSD.* New York: Guilford Press.

van der Kolk, B.A., McFarlane, A.C. and Weisaeth, L. (eds) (1996) *Traumatic Stress: The Effects of Overwhelming Experience on Mind, Body and Society.* New York: Guilford Press.

Wilson, J.P. and Raphael, B. (eds) (1993) *International Handbook of Traumatic Stress Syndromes.* New York: Plenum Press.

Chapter 5

Vicarious traumatization

Professionals who risk their lives in the course of their jobs are a source of interest to the media in general, and often their work is made to look adventurous, challenging and attractive. Yet not only would much of the work of the emergency services be considered unfit for public viewing, but also their work is often undertaken in a critical, hostile and verbally aggressive arena (Miletich 1990). Working with dangerous and potentially life-threatening incidents while at the centre of public gaze and as the subject of intense scrutiny can compound the stress of the event. The behaviour of the public can often impede the work of the emergency services, leaving them frustrated as they struggle to control the whole situation. This is illustrated in a police officer's account of the scene of an accident:

> A woman had been knocked down and killed by a young male driver. A crowd of onlookers were verbally abusing the driver of the car and threatening him. In trying to restore some order I then became the focus of their abuse and everyone began to pitch in, complaining about having warned the police that an accident was waiting to happen on this road. The whole situation quickly became dangerous and out of control and in the midst of it I'm struggling to deal respectfully with the dead woman lying at the centre of the scene.

Stress in emergency service work

The nature of emergency service work can involve exposure to high adrenalin life-threatening situations interspersed with prolonged periods of relative calm and potential boredom. In addition, organization-based stressors, such as negative interpersonal relationships and work overload, remain a significant source of stress in the emergency services. However, the nature of the traumatic incidents with which emergency personnel work on a daily basis can compound the work-related stress experienced.

Threat of physical injury and exposure to life and death medical emergencies in often potentially hazardous public environments have been found to add significantly to the stress of the job. Specific traumatic incidents such as major fires and accidents involving babies and children have been found to incur psychological distress in a high percentage of paramedics and firecrew alike (Thompson and Suzuki 1991; Ravenscroft 1993; Bryant and Harvey 1996). Dealing, repeatedly, with the death of young children and with bereavement are reported to be major sources of stress within the police service (Hetherington and Munro 1997).

The majority of emergency service personnel involved in critical incidents are found to have, at some time in their career, experienced post traumatic stress reactions (Mitchell and Bray 1990; Raphael and Wilson 1994). The majority will recover and develop more effective coping strategies to assist them in dealing with the job. For some, the intrusive imagery and other symptoms characteristic of PTSD remain with them and interfere with their normal everyday functioning, both at work and at home.

A major factor in the development of post traumatic stress reactions in the fire service and ambulance service has been found to be the repeated experience of routine incidents of a traumatic nature (Fitzpatrick 1994; Tyler and Leather 1999). Frequent exposure of police officers and accident and emergency staff to small scale traumatic incidents has been recognized as having a cumulative effect, often referred to as *sequential traumatization* (Hetherington 1993; Peters-Bean 2000). The cumulative nature of the smaller scale traumatic events may increase the 'unexpectedness' of the individual's reactions because they may have coped previously with more serious accidents without exhibiting adverse reactions. Yet the frequency with which such events occur can aggravate the processing of preceding trauma, and intensify the characteristic reactions to traumatic incidents.

An appreciation of the effects of traumatic incidents on ourselves is fundamental to our dealing with the reactions of those about us. This insight is essential to those who constantly work with critical incidents and whose personal reactions may impact adversely on those to whom they are responding. The following case illustration demonstrates the potential for individual reactions to trauma to interfere with the effective management of others:

> The police officer stopped a 19-year-old speeding on the motorway. The young man was driving a Ford Escort, a popular choice for his age group, a fast yet inexpensive model. He was invited into the police car and duly admonished. He appeared courteous, remorseful and concerned at being stopped. The police officer was visibly disturbed by the offence. His anger towards the driver was evident. He found it difficult to calm his level of arousal following the incident, and continued to replay the event, together with the many others of a similar nature to which he had responded. In the majority, the similar incidents had ended in tragedy, and this police officer had witnessed the mutilation and death of those involved. He had dealt with the bereavement of the families in the aftermath. The officer had repressed his own anger towards the frequently young and inexperienced drivers who had caused the incidents and themselves paid dearly through their own injury or death. In response to the present driver he struggled to control his reactions, the accumulation of feelings towards many others.

Traumatic stress at work

A knowledge and awareness of the potential effects of constant exposure to traumatic incidents is essential in the effective use of counselling skills with the public, in the supervision of employees and in the provision of peer support within the emergency service. This chapter examines the specific effects of constant exposure to smaller scale traumatic incidents which are the substance of the emergency service employee's work. The DSM IV criteria for PTSD form the framework by which the descriptions of emergency service worker's reactions to routine traumatic incidents are discussed (APA 1994). While DSM IV provides a suitable template for the identification of the characteristic reactions which constitute PTSD, most individuals experiencing these reactions to varying extents will not go on to develop post traumatic stress disorder.

A core criterion for a critical incident is the experience of an event which constitutes a threat to life or limb in self or others. Regular exposure to life-threatening situations is commonplace in emergency service work and can incur severe stress reactions, reducing an individual's feeling of invulnerability, and generating haunting fears of imminent death (Peterson *et al.* 1991). The normal reactions which an individual, exposed to a traumatic incident, is likely to experience usually diminish over a four week period. During this natural period of recovery, emergency service professionals are likely in the normal course of their duties to experience a further critical incident. This can interfere with the phase of reprocessing the incident and incur a cumulative effect. The following incident describes a regular and potentially life-threatening situation which one officer experienced:

> I was on police motorcycle duty when I chased a stolen car. The car deliberately rammed me to escape . . . I was absent for 95 days. I had serious mental problems following the accident. I had recurring nightmares and no concentration. I had flashbacks when I rode a motorcycle. Overall I felt that I could not deal with the stress at work.

This description begs further information. What other factors may have contributed to the officer's experience of the incident – training, experience, operational support, current life circumstances, social support, debriefing and peer support following the event? Were procedures put in place to allow his rehabilitation to motorcycle duty? The anticipation of returning to the same role can in itself be disturbing if an individual's sense of vulnerability has been increased. A sense of guilt, shame and fear can be enduring features of such an incident if not acknowledged and processed. For most individuals experiencing a traumatic event, there is a recovery period in which it is not likely they will re-experience the same event. For the emergency service professional, there is no such natural period of recovery from trauma. They return to the job with the knowledge that the next trauma is imminent.

Research into the effects of constant exposure to smaller scale traumatic events has shown that a significant number of individuals experience reactions characteristic of post traumatic stress disorder. However, given the nature of emergency work, it is likely that at any point in time, most professionals are experiencing reactions to recent traumatic events. Yet, for some professionals certain reactions survive through time. For many the scenes, sounds or smells of traumatic events remain indelibly printed on their mind. These memories are recorded at a point of heightened awareness in the form of visual or sensory images, and can be replayed like videos (see van der Kolk *et al.* 1996 for further discussion of trauma memory). They may have lost their emotional valence through time or, if relived through their retelling, may still activate the emotional reactions experienced at the time of the event. The memories characteristically contain a high level of detail. The individual is often unable to summarize the content of the recollection but driven to retell it as witnessed at the time. The following incident is told by a police officer:

> It was a typical Sunday lunchtime. I was called to a road traffic accident. I was the first on the scene. There was a car with a woman dead at the wheel. She had been crushed and pushed so far back in the car that she had also crushed her daughter. The daughter was still alive, wedged, with her face squashed against her mother's face. She was screaming for her mother whom she knew was dead. There was no consolation for this young girl. I knew that she was so badly injured she was unlikely to survive. I sat with her while she screamed and while she died. To this day I can still hear her crying.

This vivid recollection was told by the officer some thirty years after it had happened. It was still capable of evoking strong emotion in its retelling. This effect is not unusual, and many emergency service professionals carry a battery of similar experiences of traumatic incidents which would be disturbing to anyone just in their telling. These memories which have persisted through time are often reminiscent of a period when there was very little support at all available. The natural response was one of repression, denial and avoidance promoted often by a macho culture and an organization which knew no more how to manage the disturbing events than did the individuals involved. At this time, many of the senior professionals had experienced larger scale trauma and contended with the aftermath of the cumulative effects as well as the situations allowed them.

A knowledge of the impact of trauma benefits not only those who experience deleterious effects in the present and in the future but also those who carry the wounds of past trauma. Understanding the natural sequelae of trauma promotes insight and empathy into the cognitive and emotional processes of traumatized individuals. It allows that understanding to be extended to the individual and to significant others who may not have been able to make sense of what may have appeared as at times disturbing behaviour patterns. The knowledge for some, that the source of the disturbance lies in the event and not in the person's manifest behaviour, may remain an elusive truth.

Traumatic stress reactions

While a diagnosis of PTSD requires fulfilment of a number of specific criteria, any of the characteristic traumatic reactions may endure in isolation or in various combinations. The experience of traumatic reactions in themselves does not constitute PTSD. The core reactions experienced following traumatic incidents are discussed in Chapter 4. They are examined here to demonstrate the ways in which they are experienced and compounded by the nature of emergency service work.

Recurrent and intrusive distressing recollections

A major reaction to traumatic events are recurrent and intrusive distressing recollections or disturbing dreams about the event.

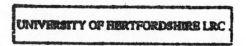

These normally take the form of scenes of the incident recurring involuntarily, such that normal thoughts are displaced by images, sounds and smells which constantly come to mind. Efforts to expel these thoughts can be exhausting and the individual may complain of the desire of release from them. The individual becomes physically tired by the incident preoccupying their waking moments. They may also recur in *disturbing dreams* and revive the feeling of re-experiencing the incident.

> I attended a fatal road traffic accident where a driver had lost control of his car while speeding and ran down a 15-year-old youth. The youth, when struck, hit his head face down on a 6-inch square wooden post, demolishing half his face. I dealt with the accident in a correct manner but following that, the first week in particular was quite harrowing. I felt embarrassed by my visible reactions to visions of the boy's face which no one else could see. I had recurring nightmares for some time afterwards, constantly seeing the youth's face, eventually waking up in a sweat. I avoided using that section of road for some time, finding an alternative route.

These intrusive thoughts can vary in intensity. They can be experienced to such an extent that the individual reacts as if back at the scene of the event, with visible physiological and emotional reactions associated with the incident. These can incur embarrassment for an emergency service professional if alone on the job. Experiences of intrusive thoughts and feelings can be so intense and overwhelming that the individual attempts to avoid anything which is remotely symbolic of the trauma.

Avoidance behaviour

Avoidance behaviour can be self-protective at certain stages in the aftermath of the trauma, in allowing the individual to exercise limited control over their recollections of the event. However, in the longer term, if avoidance behaviour is adopted in an effort to dispel the disturbing experiences from memory, then it can be counter-productive and delay the individual's recovery.

Avoidance of recollections of a traumatic event may not be immediately evident as in instances where professionals may avoid the physical scene of an accident or block out memories and thoughts associated with the incident. However, revisiting the scene of the incident is ultimately unavoidable, as in the case where the traumatic incident happens within the workplace; avoidance can still be difficult to detect if masked by sickness and absence from work. It is important that professionals are monitored through peer support or by supervisors following exposure to clearly disturbing incidents to allow symptoms of post traumatic stress, such as avoidance, to be addressed appropriately. Avoidance in the aftermath of trauma can otherwise become entrenched and be more difficult to overcome, as in the following description:

> A 10-year-old boy was dragged by a tube train until
> he hit a wall. I was told that he looked a 'mess'. When
> I pulled back the rubber sheet to label him, I saw a
> hundred different pieces of him and all identifiable as a
> young boy. I was all right outwardly. Later that day I was
> told that his mother was coming to see him as she didn't
> believe it was him. To see her distress and horror was
> unbearable. She refused to leave him and sat handling his
> body and sobbing uncontrollably. After that even joints
> of meat made me think of him. I couldn't get him out of
> my mind. I called in sick. Each time I tried going back to
> the hospital, I turned back. I should have been able to
> manage. I was trained to.

Dealing with mutilation and death

An inherent aspect of the work of the emergency services is dealing with scenes of mutilation and death. These aspects of a traumatic incident are rarely experienced in isolation but often involve the equally disturbing role of managing the distress and anguish of others at the scene or subsequently breaking the news to family members. While the professional may focus on the larger task at hand, it is often the finer details of the sensory experience which linger on and remain symbolic of the event.

These details act as triggers for the memory, which when re-experienced serve the purpose of reactivating the memory. In effect they can ensure that the memory is reprocessed to satisfaction. They can also be unwelcome reminders of the incident, the individuals involved, the invulnerability of life and so on, cascading a myriad of thoughts in the professional which dwarf the significance of their current experience. It is often this trigger effect which incurs the longer term sequelae of depression and anxiety, fuelled by the professional's perceived need to adopt socially acceptable behaviour, and to protect others from negative thoughts and feelings. The following description demonstrates how the mutilation resulting from a road traffic accident can add to its emotional impact, while the smells and sights symbolic of the scene continue to revive memories of the incident.

> I went to a RTA where a man was trapped in a vehicle.
> The car had suddenly caught fire and we weren't able to
> get him out. It was my first failed rescue. I watched him
> burn alive. After that day I was unable to eat red meat or
> anything resembling it. The smell of cooked meat and
> the sight of it acts as an immediate deterrent. Barbecues
> are never welcome events.

Diminishing sense of invulnerability

Experience of traumatic incidents diminish the sense of invulnerability which people normally hold. Emergency service workers, in their constant exposure to incidents of death and mutilation, are unable to preserve a sense that they and their family members will survive against the odds. For them death and injury are realities which they encounter on a daily basis. Thus, fears relating to their safety or that of family members are uppermost in their mind. These fears can be sustained by intrusive thoughts and images in which the real victims of events with which the professionals have dealt are superimposed on images of members of the professional's own family. These images at the time can be vivid and disturbing. These intrusive images can reinforce a sense of impending danger which is not shared by others. Individuals exposed to traumatic incidents often adopt protective behaviours in anticipation of their death or injury. Preparing for their families' welfare through writing wills or discussing at length how their family would cope in their absence is to some extent motivated by the emergency service professional's personality of protecting others, especially those dependent on them. Equally, these feelings are easily stimulated if family members are not accounted for. Emergency service professionals may find it difficult to tolerate not having information on a significant other's whereabouts. The professional in such a situation can be haunted by images of the other's fate. Horrific and highly disturbing images and scenes of the individual monopolize the professional's thoughts. The other is not perceived as 'late', but imagined dead or mutilated, and by the most horrendous means. These harrowing thoughts are sufficiently vivid and live for the family member on returning to be confronted with an avalanche of feelings which may now bear little relation to the real event encountered. Yet for the professional, those imagined thoughts reflect the other's importance and the extent of the potential loss which they experience on a daily basis.

Identifying with victims or their family

Any factors which increase the identification with the victim or their family can also increase the officer's vulnerability to the impact of the event. This reaction is frequently experienced by emergency service personnel when similarities appear between the victim and the helper's own personal life circumstances. This makes it more difficult for professionals to dissociate from the incident, to retain an emotional distance and to focus on a sense of their positive role in the rescue and recovery of the incident. It immediately short-circuits natural defences by accessing thoughts of those family members for whose protection they feel responsible. Psychologically, images of them as being harmed invade the professional's thoughts. The incident has served to stimulate underlying fears of loss and devastation over which now, even in their mind, they may not be able to exercise any control. Subsequently, intrusive thoughts and images associated with the event are triggered by everyday objects that are symbolic of the traumatic incident and can evoke intense psychological distress. A professional describes an experience which involves identification with the victim's family:

> A 9-year-old male pedal cyclist was run over and completely crushed, mutilated and killed by a large truck at a roundabout. The boy's mother arrived at the scene, by chance, minutes afterwards just as I arrived, and collapsed and became hysterical . . . I dealt with the accident and on arriving home late, having been delayed by the accident, I burst out crying on seeing my own son of the same age. I couldn't sleep that night. Every time I pass the scene I think about the accident and see the scene again in my mind. Although I am no longer upset by it, I was at the time, and was for some weeks afterwards.

Being able to express overwhelming feelings of distress and anger immediately and openly in an accepting environment can help the processing of the event. The presence of social support can buffer the effects of traumatic incidents, but it can equally compound the stress of the event. Frequently individuals experiencing traumatic incidents are unable to disclose the details of the event to others close to them. This may be due to the maintenance of self-image, a desire to protect others from the horrible nature of the incident, or a feeling that if others have not been there they will not understand. However, social support where available should not detract from the organizational responsibility to provide appropriate support from within the organization in the form of debriefings, formal peer support and supportive working environment.

Sense of helplessness

A sense of helplessness can add to the impact of the event. Situations in which officers are unable to take any action can reduce their sense of control, and heighten the emotional impact of the incident they are forced to witness. This can increase the personal sense of guilt and feelings of inadequacy that they should have done more. These feelings of responsibility for rescue attempts that fail are often intensified by their contact with the remaining family, who seek out details of the death and of the emergency service worker's role. The following description demonstrates the sense of helplessness aggravated by the images of young children and their dependency on the emergency service professional for their survival:

> A family of four died in their car. There was nothing that could be done to get them out until the Fire Brigade arrived, which was some time after our arrival on the scene. I believe that the two adults in the front of the car may have died instantly in the head-on crash with a lorry. The two children in the back were clearly alive. Deeply shocked, their eyes fixed on me through the windows, as I tried desperately to get in. As the flames suddenly began to lap around the vehicle, the look on their faces wracked in disbelief, pain and anguish will always stay with me. You don't get over something like that.

In this situation, there is little to reframe positively. The professional was cast in the role of witness to a disaster. He was there prior to its unfolding and was rendered impotent by the nature of the event. He was reminded of the limits of his capacity to rescue, concerns over his contribution, questioning if he could have done anything further. Following the event, he was left only with a deep seated sense of despair.

Feelings of guilt

As with the immediate victims of traumatic incidents, emergency service professionals are likely to experience feelings of guilt. The core personality attributes of emergency professionals, a personal sense of commitment, control, responsibility and a pride in the outcome of their efforts can lead them to scrutinize their own contributions to the outcome of an event. In most instances, these emergent feelings of guilt are founded on incidental events which may not have directly contributed to a negative outcome, such as the route taken to the scene of an accident, limited resources to cater for the survival of all the victims, questions about decisions taken at the time in the light of new information. And where the decisions or actions of professionals do appear to have contributed to further pain, suffering or even death they can leave the professional with a resounding and real sense of guilt. This is illustrated in the following senior house officer's description of a misdiagnosis:

> A grossly neglected child was admitted to A and E. I
> misdiagnosed her as being leukaemic. In fact she had
> suffered a non-accidental head injury. Left alone later
> with her parents, she suffered further injuries. Had
> this not then have been recognized by a senior nurse,
> she could have been killed. As it was, she suffered
> unnecessary pain and injury and my neglect of her too.

The persistence of these feelings of guilt can impede the professional's recovery from the impact of the event and undermine their subsequent performance on the job. In the majority of cases, such feelings are unlikely to be founded in reality, but are likely to be a natural consequence of exposure to a traumatic incident resulting in death or serious injury. It is important that, in formally reviewing procedures and practices following traumatic events, professionals also receive psychological debriefing to reframe the course of events as they occurred and realistically evaluate their own contribution to them.

Anger

Anger is a characteristic reaction to traumatic incidents, where individuals feel a sense of outrage at the needless loss of life. Often there is no safe outlet for these feelings. Those involved in or responsible for the traumatic events have usually also suffered as a result of the incident. Generally emergency service workers are left to contain their outrage. These feelings of anger coupled with a sense of helplessness may be directed at the employing organization or the legal system. Police officers in particular can feel angry about a system of justice which they see as insufficient in dealing with those who have needlessly caused death or injury to another person. These feelings are reflected in the following description:

> I attended a fatal RTA involving an 8-year-old girl and her mother. Both died. I held the girl in my arms as she died. There was nothing that could be done to save her or her mother. The guilty party was not even prosecuted because of a delay in serving the summons. A lot of work for nothing. I felt I couldn't do justice to the dependants.

Feeling angry is often an appropriate response to a traumatic incident. When verbalized it can be effective in helping to process associated feelings. The organization is frequently an impersonal and safe lightning conductor for latent feelings of anger, feelings that may be founded in reality. They may also be fuelled by an individual's personal post trauma reactions, where the organization may be perceived as inadequate in its protective and caring capacity. Feelings of transference can be experienced towards institutions. For example, at times of heightened sensitivity, the organization may be experienced as a parental figure lacking in responsibility for the individual's welfare. For the emergency services which promote the effective management of the public's feelings of conflict and anger, the containment of adverse reactions should be assumed as a cultural norm.

Research into the nature of traumatic events highlights the prevalent characteristics of the event which serve to increase the indelibility of the incident in the individual's memory and to preserve the enduring sounds, sights and smells of the traumatic scene way beyond the event itself. The characteristics of the event may be further compounded by individual vulnerability factors and inadequate organizational interventions following traumatic incidents, prolonging the individual's unwelcome experience of post traumatic stress reactions. The growing knowledge of the effects of traumatic incidents on the psychological functioning of individuals enables intervention strategies to be tailored to maximize the natural and specific recovery resources of the individual (see Figley 1995). For emergency service professionals, who constantly manage the traumas of others, the provision of refined and specialist intervention strategies is paramount both to their psychological well-being, to retaining them as a trained and competent workforce, and in helping them to use their own experiences through the use of counselling skills with others.

Emergency service personnel are a valuable resource in the aftermath of trauma, not only for the public but also to each other. When trained to use counselling skills to support colleagues they can be instrumental in enabling them to cope with trauma and other work-related difficulties. The nature and value of peer support at work is discussed in the next chapter.

Further reading

Figley, C.R. (ed.) (1995) *Compassion Fatigue: Coping with Secondary Traumatic Stress Disorder in Those who Treat the Traumatised.* New York: Brunner Mazel.

Grosch, W.N. and Olsen, D.C. (1994) *Where Helping Starts to Hurt.* London: Norton.

Hodgkinson, P.E. and Stewart, M. (1991) *Coping with Catastrophe.* London: Routledge.

Chapter 6

Counselling skills in peer support

Most workers spend the majority of their adult waking lives at work. In fact, for many people a working environment and schedule are crucial for their psychological health (Warr 1987). The substance of an employee's work, the interpersonal relationships they form, and the structure and culture of the organization have considerable effect on their psychological well-being. Working life occupies a large part of an employee's thoughts. Moreover an employee's working hours impact on family life, and in turn family life affects the employee's work (Hewitt 1993). This is reflected in the following explanation of an employee's efforts to succeed at work at the expense of her personal life and ultimately her performance in the workplace:

> While working as a sister I was also asked to take charge temporarily of the department. I did the two jobs for nine months, until I felt I could no longer cope. I spoke to management who told me I was now permanently in the senior role. Because of the hours I had spent trying to run two posts while my initial post was filled, my health suffered, my home life suffered, and I'm sure my colleagues in the department suffered from my moods.

The cumulative effect of both home and work pressures can interfere with an employee's ability to perform effectively in the workplace. Increased awareness of absenteeism, sickness, early retirement and turnover have raised organizational awareness of the underlying causal variables. Although emotional and psychological support of workmates has always been present within the profession, there has been a concerted effort of late by organizations to refine and develop the support proffered to personnel. In part this is due to the recognition of the value of such a resource for employees, particularly in the event of traumatic incidents. Furthermore, it fulfils a number of goals for an organization in promoting the employee's return to full occupational performance following work-related psychological difficulties. Support is most frequently provided in the form of counselling through internal employee assistance programmes delivered by welfare departments, occupational health or in-house counsellors. These services may also be supplemented by the use of an external consultant counsellor or a full external employee assistance programme. In the United States and more recently in the UK, formal peer support programmes have been developed to provide additional support to employees. In the UK, these are normally operated as an extension and supplement to internal welfare services.

Peer support

Peer support skills refers to the trained and informed use of counselling skills within an organization by selected employees at all levels for the purpose of providing support for colleagues. For the emergency services, this involves designated employees, primarily trained to 'help' the public, also employing their skills to the benefit of their colleagues. A peer support system entails a rigorous selection procedure, specialist training and supervision. This system requires continued monitoring to ensure the well-being of emergency personnel receiving and providing support. Peer support personnel may perform the following tasks:

- being available to peers who have been involved in disturbing traumatic incidents
- identifying individuals who may need peer support or professional referral

- participating as required in defusings or debriefings
- providing on-scene support services when necessary
- assisting in occupational and traumatic stress educational activities.

Peer support personnel

The selection of appropriate employees to train for peer support must be rigorous. While there is no research evidence to support the selection of specific characteristics, there are particular factors which would act as contra-indicators in respect of certain individuals. For instance, employees who seek training in peer support may be driven by their own experience of trauma, and by their empathy and insight to the aftermath of feelings resulting from the traumatic incident. While it can be advantageous for employees to have experience of trauma and its repercussions, it is essential that they have processed their own traumas. Traumatic reactions can incur prolonged avoidance feelings, leading individuals, still preoccupied by the trauma, to submerge themselves in others' feelings in an effort to avoid processing their own. Equally, the intention to help others may be a reflection of the individual's natural coping mechanism, in transforming the personal experience of trauma into a positive outcome, by using the experience productively in an effort to help others.

As employees within the emergency services are characteristically energized, familiar with trauma and driven to help others in crisis, selecting individuals who have overcome personal experiences of trauma is best conducted through structured assessment by appropriate professionals. Organizations selecting and training peer support employees have a responsibility to ensure that the employee selected is not currently in the process of recovering from post traumatic stress. Following selection, the organization must ensure that peer support employees are not likely to become vicariously traumatized in carrying out their support role. This can be avoided by ongoing training, systematic debriefing and supervision by suitably qualified professionals.

The task of employees formally fulfilling dual roles is inherently problematic. Immediate issues such as qualifications, confidentiality and ethics arise, together with the legal implications of these matters for the organization. For example, if an officer seeks peer support from a supervisor for a personal problem which may potentially be impeding their performance at work, the supervisor often has a duty not only to the officer, but also to their colleagues, and to the public at large to ensure its safety. Such a situation can compromise confidentiality. The role conflict created by such dilemmas can limit the support that can be provided. It is important that when peer support is formally implemented that there are stringent considerations of confidentiality and that these should be made explicit to all concerned. Equally it cannot always be assumed that because a profession is people-oriented and uses counselling skills as part of the job, that it is necessarily best placed to provide formal support for its own members. It can be a suitable compromise that peer support is provided across bases or across the different emergency services.

Rationale for peer support

While there are significant implications to an organization in the operation of a formal peer support programme, there are equally many advantages to be gained by readily accessible support from colleagues who are fully acquainted with the nature of the job and the working climate. This point is echoed by Hughes (1991), who believes that the availability of the counsellor and the normality of the context plays an important part in the outcome. Stewart (1979: 18), writing from an NHS background, argues that counselling should not be 'hived off' to specialists because there is a need to 'deal with the action where it originates'. This is perhaps illustrated in one police officer's description of a harrowing incident:

> There was a man moving. He looked as if he was still alive. He was still moving. They stopped me going to him. They assured me later that he was already dead. His body was moving as it dried out. I broke down at the scene. The sergeant took me in the patrol car and had a stiff drink. These incidents you never forget.

This officer recounted this incident many years after the event. This had been one of his first experiences in the police force which had stayed with him. The impact of the event had no doubt been modified by his sergeant's spontaneous support. The traumatic experience had not prevented the police officer's commitment to the force, nor his subsequent successful career within it. The sergeant's empathy and support at the time had enabled the officer to accept his own reactions to the event, and in the years to come, as a senior officer he was able to acknowledge similar feelings in others. In the past, the provision of support has not always been valued by organizations.

Frequently, an ethos of individual coping has prevailed with many senior officers subscribing to a 'macho' culture, on the grounds that they survived themselves without the need for support from others. Yet coping is a precarious skill. Circumstances which may occur at different times in individuals' lives (as discussed in Chapter 5) may render them vulnerable to the impact of traumatic events to which they would otherwise be resilient. At such a juncture, the absence of support compounds the employee's reactions to the event, fuelling a discontent with the organization for whom he or she has risked personal injury, as illustrated in the following police officer's experience:

> I was on police motorcycle duty when I chased a stolen car. The car deliberately rammed me to escape; as a result, I lost all my front teeth and sustained a neck injury. I was absent from work for four months. I had serious mental problems following the accident, recurring nightmares, constant lapses in attention, flashbacks on riding my bike. I had no help at all from the police with my mental problems. Returning to work, I felt unable to deal with the stress.

Threat to life can commonly incur severe psychological reactions as devastating as any physical injuries incurred (Soloman *et al.* 1990). While usually there is adequate provision for *physical* injury in the emergency services, recognition of the injury incurred by the *psychological* impact of traumatic events is relatively recent. Unless a working environment is cultivated which accepts an employee's temporary inability to cope, then the individual often attempts to conceal their difficulties in the workplace from those who are in a position to help them. Thus management can often be the last to hear of employee problems that may be undermining both individual and organizational performance. Prior to the implementation of peer support within the organization, it is imperative that a culture is promoted in which there is no stigma attached to seeking help. Similarly, if employees providing peer support hold prejudiced views, their feelings will be detected by individuals seeking help and will prevent the uptake of support. Perceptions of organizational culture formed early in a professional's career can be difficult to reverse, as illustrated in the following case:

> I arrived at the scene of a road traffic accident. One victim was trapped in his car, unconscious. I can still see the second victim glued to the road in congealed blood, and having to lift him off the road by his legs, which were shattered. The legs felt like jelly. Apparently I had asked why the ambulance crew were not trying to revive him. I feel embarrassed about it now. I can see it all like yesterday. I've never really talked about it until now. No one is bothered work-wise. There is always a worse situation.

The value of peer support

Deriving support from colleagues has long since been recognized as beneficial (Reese *et al.* 1990). It is often reported by individuals experiencing traumatic stress reactions that only someone who had undergone the same event was able to appreciate the aftermath of feelings. The work of the emergency services exposes employees to events that are outside the range of most individuals' experience. The commonality of the job enables trained peer support employees to provide immediate support, and this, coupled with supervision and professional referral services, creates an effective support system.

Without this form of immediate and ongoing support from fellow officers, many professionals would be unable to do the job at all. The need for support in protecting the professional's psychological welfare, and in maintaining their commitment to and satisfaction of their job, is evidenced in the following fire officer's experience:

> We carried three burnt bodies from the embers, two unrecognizable, both of children under 5, and one of an asphyxiated older woman. I can still vividly see the scene and hear the ringing and tormented screams of the mother, a single parent who had lost her mother and her children. In the following days, the sound of my own young children laughing made me think of the scene and the mother's anguish. It would leave me paralysed in thought. The greatest horror was the images that sprung into my mind of my own children dead and burnt. It increased my fear that they would get hurt, as if the images themselves might make it happen. You can't talk to your family about things like that. You can only talk to someone who's seen it and lived it.

The impact of a traumatic event on emergency service workers and the beneficial effects of peer support are well documented. Yet many of the stresses experienced by employees can be unrelated to traumatic incidents. These can be occupational pressures experienced in most professions, such as work overload, underload, management pressure, unnecessary paperwork, and so on. These sources of stress are familiar to peer support employees. Reactions to stress are often more readily recognized objectively by those other than the individual concerned. An understanding of the symptoms of stress, together with an awareness of the individual factors that may at any time predispose an employee to become stressed, are important for the peer support employee. While at such times it might be innappropriate to intervene, being aware and available might be all that is necessary. The traumatic nature of the working environment can make standard work stress all the more frustrating, as illustrated in this nurse's reaction to the ongoing stress within a casualty department:

> The greatest cause of stress I feel is ignorance, with no support on decisions in which I don't feel confident or

competent in making. This coupled with the number of
agency nurses who don't know the department and the
constant flow of patients increases the workload and
personal sense of responsibility.

The internal systematic provision of peer support can often be
the only effective support immediately available for professionals whose families may not be able to proffer an informed and
specialist perspective on the workplace event causing the disturbance. Together with formal peer support programmes, the trained
use of counselling skills by senior staff in their supervisory capacity can be instrumental in restoring an individual's normal
workplace functioning following a disturbing incident at work.
For instance, a senior house officer, who is disturbed by a personal misdiagnosis of a patient, here refers to the value of support from a senior member of the department in reframing the
experience in a constructive way:

> I nearly sent a patient home. Only the fact that he
> started vomiting on leaving made me admit him to the
> A and E ward. An hour later his symptoms worsened. He
> required emergency surgery for a ruptured spleen and
> internal bleeding. How could I have missed that? Senior
> staff were reassuring. They emphasized the shared
> responsibilities for misjudgements and the standard
> process of reviewing potential errors to prevent them
> from being counter-productive.

Accessibility of peer support

Senior management can find themselves excluded from peer support. There are few peers of a similar status in their particular
organization, and seeking support from those for whom they
fulfil a management role can be anathema to them. This isolation from support can compound the inherent stresses of the
job. In the following illustration, a sister within an A and E
department describes the pressure she felt to manage the distress
of the job alone:

In a position of seniority, it's easy to feel foolish admitting to junior staff that you are upset, mainly in the instances of bereavement. A feeling of admitting something lacking. There quite often isn't a senior person around in that situation.

The lack of availability of others within the organization who are in an equivalent position can serve to isolate managers from the culture of support which they promote. While support may be available from others in a similar role in a different region, this is not necessarily as accessible, and may be compromised by fear of organizational politics. One employee at senior management level admits:

It's like a jungle at the top. There isn't anyone to talk to. In my position, people are waiting for me to pass on, to make a mistake, to get knocked off so that my job comes free. The politics are cut-throat. You can't talk to the guy who's working for you, and you can't talk to the guy you're working for. You'd be giving people ammunition to use against you.

While peer support is more commonly available among operational levels of employees, counselling skills can be effectively employed at all levels within the organization. Fowler (1991) contends that counselling skills have a central role in both management competence and training, and that appropriate training should be incorporated into all supervisory and management programmes. This view is echoed by Arroba and James (1988), referring to the police force, who feel that training in counselling skills heightens management's sensitivity to the stresses they themselves may impose on their employees. An increased awareness of how management systems and style can be a major source of stress can lead to a proactive response to that stress.

Counselling skills in management

In the UK, it is normally assumed that those in a supervisory role will exercise a responsibility for the welfare of their staff, although they may receive little training and may be poorly suited for such a role. Understanding and maintaining good relationships with staff is fundamental to managerial expertise. What destroys a relationship is the sense that the supervisor does not have the time, does not listen or is not interested. The effective use of counselling skills can help to avert these negative feelings. Carroll (1995: 23–9), writing on the use of counselling skills by management, suggests that it 'increases their ability to deal more easily and quickly with employee issues, to recognise signs of distress or disturbance more quickly and to be able to relate to their staff in more humane ways'. In relation to work tasks, counselling skills are powerful tools in facilitating others to resolve problems, and empowering them to take responsibility. This can feel uncomfortable to a controlling management style accustomed to making all the decisions, with little confidence in the workforce to act responsibly, often termed 'macho-management' (Dutfield and Ealing 1990). Yet there is strong evidence to suggest that the use of counselling skills in managing people not only leads to a healthier workforce but also increases overall performance.

When management do use counselling skills, it is important that the distinction between the levels of competence in their dual roles is made explicit. As Nixon and Carroll (1994: 7) note, 'Managers cannot be counsellors but need to build up their counselling skills in order to be fully effective in their roles'. The crucial boundary to be made explicit at the onset is that while a manager will try to help an employee with their problem, there are limits to what the employee or manager should disclose. That is, if the employee reveals information which could compromise their working relationship, then it is best not disclosed. But if an employee discloses personal information which is clearly against the organization's policy or which might interfere with the employee's workplace functioning, such as accessing pornography on the Internet or substance abuse, there would be a clear duty of disclosure.

To avoid the misuse of counselling skills within a management role, the limits to confidentiality that are possible should be clearly stated prior to any potential disclosures being made. However, in some interactions which call upon the use of counselling skills by a manager, information subsequently disclosed may not have been anticipated. The following case illustrates the role conflict arising when an employee requests a discussion with her manager relating to a prospective promotion.

> I discussed with the head of my department my
> prospective promotion, my commitment to the job, and
> intention to pursue my career in the profession. He was
> easy to talk to and very quickly, I began to tell him of
> the disturbing pressure I was under from my husband
> who wanted me to start a family, and that while I may
> have to succumb to the pressure, I would intend to
> return to my career.

The role conflict here has arisen because the employee has disclosed a personal problem which creates conflict for the supervisor beyond those that had been anticipated. Although the manager may have supported the employee's promotion, he now has to consider if he can warrant promoting and retraining her at the company's expense if there is a prospect that she may soon leave. Their working relationship has now been compromised by their joint knowledge of the tenuous situation. As a trusted adviser to her, he also feels responsible for the predicament. The unwelcome knowledge jeopardizes his credibility, the performance of the department, and his relationship with the employee and the team.

These problems could have been avoided if the supervisor had begun by clarifying the boundaries of the session, explaining that no disclosure should be made which might compromise his role as her working manager. Following the initial clarification, it is important for a manager to continue to monitor the ensuing interaction, retaining control and being prepared to interject if the focus is lost. If a manager becomes aware that there may be underlying issues which might have an impact on the employee's workplace functioning, then the manager should be in a position to refer the individual on for professional counselling. In this way, managers are able to respond appropriately to the employee's needs while fulfilling their professional responsibility to their organizations.

Caution in the use of counselling skills

Counselling skills when effective by practitioners can be a powerful tool, lulling individuals into a sense of security in which they sometimes lose all feelings of caution. Because the individual becomes engrossed in the content of the story and its associated feelings, and because of the vulnerability experienced in seeking help, it is essential that a supervisor maintains appropriate boundaries. This involves remaining sufficiently detached from content to pay conscious attention to emotional valence while monitoring content which may threaten role conflict. To this end, an individual employing counselling skills at work must be trained in:

• delivering cautions around disclosure
• recognizing when boundaries are in danger of being crossed
• being knowledgeable about when continuing to employ counselling skills would be unethical
• adopting appropriate alternative courses of action if the boundary is in jeopardy.

It is equally important for those using counselling skills to be able to identify employees who might be more appropriately referred to a professional counsellor (see Chapter 4). Megranahan (1994) considers that referral skills fail often because the manager does not recognize the need for referral and persists in counselling in a situation in which they are neither adequately trained nor competent. This applies equally to both peer supporters and to mental health professionals working in the emergency services. Gist and Woodall (1995) make the point that 'good fences make good neighbours – psychologists who want to play firefighter and firefighters who want to play psychologist are both dangers to themselves and others'. For the manager or peer support employee, recognizing the limitations of their expertise, skills and competence is essential to the well-being of the employee who has entrusted their feelings in them (see Chapter 2). The employee in a state of distress or anger is often not in a position to discern adequately what they need, therefore it is important that the helper contains the situation and is aware of how and where to make appropriate referrals, all the time maintaining confidentiality. Additional support may be in the form of an internal welfare service, an employee assistance programme or consultant psychologist or counsellor.

The use of counselling skills with personnel experiencing work-related difficulties cannot be considered to be a panacea.

They cannot create contented and committed workers, since the individual's values and choices remain at the focus of the process. In fact, at times it can lead to employees making decisions which might not meet with the approval of management (Einzig and Evans 1990). However, training in the use of counselling skills in the aftermath of trauma remains a significant means by which the professional can be supported through the strength, insight and empathy of a peer who has personal experience of the job. This experience, informed by a knowledge of the physiological, emotional and psychological impact of trauma, maximizes the impact of counselling skills. It enables the skills to be used effectively to promote empathy, to normalize the individual's reactions and to facilitate individual coping behaviours. The use of counselling skills by management and by peers can go a long way towards creating a healthy working environment and promoting a supportive culture in which the organization demonstrates a responsibility for the stress experienced by its employees as a result of the jobs they do.

Central to the professional use of counselling skills within any organization is a fundamental knowledge of the legal and ethical implications of their practice. The next chapter addresses these issues with reference to current law and recommended codes of conduct.

Further reading

Carroll, M. (1996) *Workplace Counselling: A Systematic Approach to Employee Care.* London: Sage.

Feltham, C. (1996) *The Gains of Listening: Perspectives on Counselling at Work.* Buckingham: Open University Press.

MacLennan, N. (1996) *Counselling for Managers.* Aldershot: Gower.

Macwhinnie, L. (1998) *An Anthology of Counselling at Work.* Rugby: Association for Counselling at Work.

Plas, J.N. and Hoover-Dempsey, K.V. (1988) *Working up a Storm: Anger, Anxiety, Joy and Tears on the Job – and How to Handle Them.* New York: Norton.

Chapter 7

Legal and ethical implications in the use of counselling skills

Organizations have a statutory responsibility for their employees' psychological well-being (Health and Safety Executive 1995). This covers the roles that emergency employees undertake with the public and those required of them in their capacity as formal peer supporters. Direct exposure to traumatic events, vicarious exposure to colleagues' traumas through peer support or exposure to inappropriate peer support all carry legal implications for the organization, as well as psychological implications for the individuals concerned. Implicit in the legitimate and therapeutic use of counselling skills is a knowledge of the boundaries of practice in terms of skills, training and ethics.

Employees using counselling skills within the parameters of a primary profession are governed by the code of conduct and responsibilities of their primary profession. In addition, they are subject to the code of ethics and practice pertaining to the professional use of counselling skills. At times, the two sets of professional codes of practice may pose ethical and legal dilemmas for the professional. For this reason, issues relating to standards, ethics and litigation need to be clarified and made explicit within the respective emergency profession both to the employee and to the individuals accessing support. The responsibility for clarity and communication of ethical, professional and legal boundaries lies with the employing organization and its employees using counselling skills in either a public or a peer capacity.

The legal context of psychological well-being in the workplace

The Health and Safety at Work Act 1995 requires that employers must ensure as 'far as is reasonably practicable' the health, safety and welfare at work of their employees (Section 2(1) of the HSW Act, IRB Bulletin 1995; Health and Safety at Work Act 1995: the Act outlines HSC2; Health and Safety Regulation: A short guide: HSC13). This duty applies to both the physical and psychological well-being of employees. There are no grounds for any distinction between physical and psychiatric injury as different kinds of injury. In addition, the Management of Health and Safety at Work regulations (Health and Safety Commission 1997) assign a statutory duty on employers to carry out risk assessments on the substance of their employees' work. The purpose of this is to ensure that employers appropriately identify potential hazards to employees' physical and psychological health: that is, who is at risk of harm, how often this occurs, and how it occurs. In this way, the extent and frequency of risk to employees can be assessed; and either the hazard removed or preventive and protective measures implemented to ensure the employee's safety.

Claims for psychological injury by employees are normally restricted to primary victims, who have been directly affected by the work-related incident as a result of their immediate, personal involvement. This involvement must have resulted in a recognized psychiatric illness. However, while the current legislation may allow personal injury claims for psychiatric illness as a result of both isolated events and prolonged exposure to events of a more frequent nature such as bullying, there is little evidence available on the frequency or success of such claims (Health and Safety Executive 1998). Of the small percentage of claims reported in the category of workplace stress, the main source of claims were for workplace bullying and the most frequent injury was reported to be 'nervous breakdown' (Earnshaw and Cooper 1996).

Damages to emergency service employees are usually restricted to physical injuries, with the assumption that dealing with disturbing and traumatic incidents is the nature of the job. However, police officers who developed post traumatic stress disorder as a result of their involvement in the Hillsborough football stadium disaster were awarded financial compensation (*Guardian*, 4 June 1996). An essential requirement for the award of compensation is that it would be reasonably foreseeable that the plaintiff might develop a psychiatric disorder as a result of the defendant's negligence (Jenkins 1997). This outcome emphasizes organizational responsibility to provide appropriate interventions to reduce the debilitating effects of such experiences.

The case of John Walker, a social worker who successfully took legal action against his employer for stress-induced psychiatric illness, is regarded as a landmark decision in terms of defining the employer's responsibility for their employee's welfare. John Walker suffered two nervous breakdowns while working for Northumberland County Council. The court decided that the employer could not be held responsible for the occurrence of the employee's initial nervous breakdown, which was unforeseeable. The outcome of the case was based on the employer's failure to take appropriate remedial action in response to the employee's first nervous breakdown. The court ruled that interventions on the part of the employers to reduce the workload would have averted his subsequent nervous breakdown (British Association of Social Workers (BASW) 1995). Cooper (1995: 14) argues that as a result of the Walker case, 'employers have a duty of care over the management of people'. Consequently, liability and legal responsibility in relation to psychiatric illness remain a source of concern to employers.

In view of current regulations, any proactive measures implemented by the employer, such as debriefing, peer support and specialist counselling, could be seen to be instrumental in ensuring the employee's psychological well-being in light of the risks they encounter on the job. However, where these measures involve their own employees, as in the provision of peer support, then the employer is again responsible for the 'safety' of the support provided, both in terms of the provider and the recipient of the support. Employers hold a vicarious liability for any acts carried out by their employees. Should the formal arrangement for the use of counselling skills in the provision of peer support incur psychological damage to the recipient, an action for negligence could be brought against the organization.

Case: vicarious traumatization

Jerry was a full time police officer who had been selected to train as a peer supporter. He was engaged in providing support for a young fellow officer who had attended a road traffic incident in which two children similar in age to his own had died. Jerry listened to the details of the incident, the officer's feelings of guilt and helplessness and his identification with the bereaved relatives. He listened to the officer's distress at the haunting noise of the children's screams. His support of the officer was instrumental in the officer's recovery. Supervision for Jerry himself was unavailable at the time due to the current demand for counselling and debriefing. One evening he returned home to the sound of his children fighting and shouting. The older child began to scream uncontrollably in temper. Jerry was overcome with rage and anger towards the child and struggled to control his wrath. He was left feeling overwhelmed by the strength of his feelings. He saw his GP and was off work for a period of four weeks.

This case demonstrates the repercussions of forgoing adequate support and supervision. Individuals providing personal support may be less likely to identify stresses in themselves and less likely to seek support and debriefing for themselves. It is the professional peer supporter's responsibility to monitor their own levels of stress and resilience and to seek supervisory support and debriefing. The point at which peer supporters begin to disregard personal support and work on relentlessly is likely to be where the individuals they are supporting mirror the same mental attitude. This kind of behaviour is referred to as parallel process, where the supporter adopts the behaviours presented by the individual seeking support. Unless recognized, the process can have an adverse effect, modelling and reinforcing the inappropriate behaviour. However, ultimately it remains the legal and ethical responsibility of the employing organization and those providing supervision not only to ensure that supervision is mandatory but also to monitor individuals for signs of vicarious traumatization.

The ethical use of counselling skills

An organization's legal responsibility for its employees' behaviour in the formal use of counselling skills does not absolve any employee from their own professional obligations and responsibilities. Professionals employing counselling skills with the public, as part of their duties, are expected to act in a way congruent with their level of training and comply with the professional and ethical requirements. The BAC *Code of Ethics and Practice for Counselling Skills* outlines the professional standards pertaining to confidentiality, anti-discriminatory practice and non-exploitative relationships (British Association of Counselling 1998). The code anticipates the problems that may arise in the use of counselling skills and provides guidelines on safe practice in the best interests of both the professional and the public. A professional code of conduct also carries implicit legal obligations (Madden 1998).

Professional ethics serve to formulate 'normative standards of conduct or actions', providing a framework for the appropriate and informed use of counselling skills (Holmes and Lindley 1994). In the main, an ethical framework is based on the concepts of autonomy, fidelity, justice, beneficence, non-maleficence and self-interest (Jenkins 1997; Bond 2000). An ethical code aims to promote the well-being and autonomy of the individual, to prevent harm to the individual or others, and to maintain the competence of the counsellor. At times, legal responsibilities may appear to conflict with ethical principles underpinning the use of counselling skills in a professional capacity. Clarifying the areas of conflict and defining explicit boundaries for the effective use of counselling skills in the context of each occupation can avoid misunderstandings that may arise.

Confidentiality and the public interest

Confidentiality is a core ethical concern in the practice of counselling skills. The legal concept of confidentiality is founded on the concept of equity, or fairness, in that an individual should not take advantage of information which was related in confidence (Reid 1986). For professionals whose primary role affords them legal authority, the issue of confidentiality is limited by reason of their conditions of employment. For the emergency services, reporting suspected child abuse is an intrinsic aspect of their professional role, and as such determines the parameters of their capacity to provide confidentiality. Hence, confidentiality afforded by emergency service employees is clearly relative to the nature of the disclosure, and is bound by the Child Protection and Terrorist Acts.

Confidentiality is normally breached only in the public interest. The public interest, as defined by the courts, proposes that confidences should be maintained and protected by law, rather than broken without due cause. Disclosure for the purpose of preventing crime is assumed to be in the public interest. In other instances, courts have widened this principle to include anti-social behaviour (Jenkins 1997). Breaches of confidentiality in this category include work-related behaviour which may be seriously compromising the employer's interest, through fraud or incompetence or by presenting a risk to themselves or to the public. For example, if an employee reports a serious alcohol problem which is undermining their competence at work to the extent that it puts the public or colleagues at risk, there would be a need for breach of confidentiality. Confidentiality would have to be broken if there was a risk of harm to self or others, for example, in an effort to prevent or reduce the risk of serious threat of suicide. There would also be a duty to warn others who may be at risk of harm, for example if an individual makes serious threats to another individual's safety. A further example of a supporter's statutory right to breach confidentiality is in the case of drug trafficking (Bond 2000).

In instances where confidentiality must be breached, a primary course of action is to seek a second professional opinion, usually from a supervisor. If it is still considered that confidentiality should be breached, then the issue has to be addressed with the individual concerned to allow them the opportunity to disclose the information voluntarily, and to understand the necessity for disclosure. The individual may decline, for instance if they are denying that there is recognizable problem, such as serious alcohol abuse in a safety sensitive occupation.

However, particularly in the case of emergency service work, discussing the issue of disclosure with the individual may not be practicable. This may be for reasons of urgency; or because of the immediate nature of the action required; or because forewarning the individual of the necessary disclosure may result in potential harm to the individual or to others. Breaking confidentiality needs to be carried out in accordance with the professional codes of conduct. This entails seeking supervision where feasible, restricting disclosure to the matter requiring disclosure, and restricting disclosure to those individuals who are in a position to act in the public interest (Sills 1997).

When using peer support skills with colleagues it is important to make explicit the limitations of confidentiality (Bond 2000). Providing an assurance of confidentiality then enables the employee to speak more openly. Yet the boundaries to confidentiality may need to be specified, not only verbally, but also in a written format. This may take the form of an information sheet which outlines the confidential nature of the interaction and the boundaries to confidentiality. Individuals in distress may not at the time hear all that is said to them, and can then be left with unnecessary concerns over the safety and privacy of what they have disclosed. Clarifying the limits of confidentiality also allows a peer support employee or manager to establish their responsibility for the limits of disclosure. It serves the purpose of preparing the employee for the occasions when the supporter may intervene to exercise a control over inappropriate disclosures.

More generally, emergency service workers, through their use of counselling skills, are privy to information of a sensitive personal nature. Members of the public, at times of high anxiety, distress or anger, may express feelings and thoughts to an emergency service worker which they might not under different circumstances. The nature of the interaction is founded on trust of the professional through their role and as a result of their skills. Assumptions of confidence may be implicit. It is important that all efforts are taken not to breach confidentiality inadvertently, for example when there is concerned enquiry by family members or friends (see British Association of Counselling 1999).

Case: breach of confidentiality

Geoffrey, a school teacher, was admitted to A and E with a serious injury which appeared to be self-inflicted. Rodney, a male nurse, talked to Geoffrey, working hard to gain his confidence and to ascertain the nature of his injuries. In the course of acknowledging his self-harm, he also confided in Rodney that it was the result of a broken relationship with a young boy. He described the boy as a very mature and experienced 15-year-old who had pursued him and was now intentionally causing him distress. Rodney acknowledged Geoffrey's anguish and went on to address the issue of the boy being under the legal age for a sexual relationship and his personal professional responsibilities in respect of the disclosure. At this point, Geoffrey denied that he had suggested either that the boy was 15 or that he was at his school. He became agitated and angry with Rodney, declaring that he had been speaking to him in confidence and how he believed that Rodney was helping him, whereas in fact Rodney was threatening to talk to the authorities about him, so jeopardizing his job and future. Geoffrey told Rodney that if he breached confidentiality and failed to substantiate his suggestions, he would take legal action against him for any damages incurred.

This case illustrates the complexities involved in relation to breach of confidentiality and public interest. Rodney would need to discuss the situation further with a supervisor and explain the needs for disclosure to Geoffrey, while referring him on for further support, given the risk of self-harm. Any decision to breach confidentiality must be taken in consultation with a supervisor or an organizational adviser and in discussion with professional bodies, who can offer an informed opinion on ethical dilemmas. Where the initial disclosure is retracted, there is always an element of risk involved in any action taken for one or other of the parties. Assessment of the balance of risk must take into account the relevant laws, the public interest and the protection of vulnerable parties, while ensuring both that value judgements are not exercised towards the offending party and that their psychological well-being in the process is given equal regard.

Access to records and disclosure of information

Keeping notes or records on peer support sessions is a further concern in the maintenance of confidentiality. Any arrangements need to be made explicit with all concerned prior to counselling skills being used in the workplace with peers. While brief notes may need to be maintained for the purpose of supervision, no identifying details should be included in them, nor should they be accessible to any unauthorized third party. Where there is peer support, the supporter may be supervised by an appropriate professional in occupational health, the welfare department or an associate health professional. It should be made explicit to any individual if their identity has to be disclosed in supervision and the extent of such disclosure. All parties involved should agree to any notes that are held. When a support service is provided by an organization, a minimum amount of data relating to overall workload and statistical summary information of those providing support may be required by the employer (Employee Assistance Professionals Association (EAPA) 1995: 22–3). Such information needs to protect the anonymity of individuals who consult the service. In the event of a referral to an external specialist, an employee receiving support needs to agree to authorize any necessary disclosure of personal information.

Individuals receiving peer support would have right of access to personal information held on them through a number of routes. If counselling records are held by welfare services, occupational health or counselling services, individuals may acquire access through the Access to Health Records Act 1990. Health records are defined as any record

> consisting of information relating to the physical or mental health of an individual who can be identified from that information, or from that and other information relating to the physical or mental health of an individual who can be identified from that information, or from that and other information in possession of the holder of the record [and] that has been made by or on behalf of the health professional in connection with the care of that individual.
>
> (Panting and Palmer 1992: 9)

It is often assumed among health professionals that there are official records which can be made available to individuals and more detailed records which can be held back for the counsellor's personal use in supervision or training. The legislation does not recognize such a distinction and individuals are entitled to access to any records held on them. However, the individual's right of access is *qualified* and *conditional* rather than absolute. Access can be declined on the basis that it may cause serious harm to the individual's mental health, for example in the event of paranoia (Jenkins 1997).

Under the Data Protection Act 1998, individuals have the right to be informed by any data user and of information about them held by the data user, and the right to be supplied with a copy of that data at a cost (Bradbury 1993). Individuals can apply to have access to computerized data records, and to have the records corrected or deleted as appropriate. It is normally assumed that any data held should be adequate, relevant and not excessive for the purpose required. Individuals are able to seek compensation through the courts if, after 11 September 1984, damage has been caused by the loss and unauthorized destruction of their personal data. If proven, a court can award compensation for any associated distress. Individuals may also claim compensation for damage caused after May 1986 as a result of inaccurate data. Access to manual records, such as those which are hand-written as opposed to computerized, are now accessible as a result of the European Community (EC) Directive 1998. This broadens an individual's right of access to files held on them still further, and carries implications for employee access to personnel or counselling files which may be in a written format (Institute for Personnel Development 1995).

Access to individual records can be gained by the police and courts under the Police and Criminal Evidence Act 1984, if there are reasonable grounds to believe that a 'serious and arrestable offence' has been committed. This includes murder, manslaughter, rape, sexual offences, firearms or explosives offences, terrorist offences or death caused by reckless driving. Right of access to therapeutic records by the police and courts, however, is excluded from police power under the Act. Authorization for seizure of such records can be obtained only by the police applying to a circuit judge (Feldman 1985).

In an emergency service, keeping notes at all is a matter of concern, where employees may be required to reveal information on a colleague in the event of internal investigations. For example, if an employee is under investigation for possible negligence, and has received formal peer support, the colleague may be required to reveal the content of any disclosures. In the event of work-related traumatic incidents which involve an internal investigation, employees are advised to consult their union representative prior to accessing peer support. Peer supporters need to be familiar with both statutory requirements and their own organizational policies in relation to the recording and disclosure of information on individuals.

Power in the use of counselling skills

In the professional use of counselling skills, it is important for the supporter to ensure that the individual's problem remains central to the interaction. It is inappropriate to disclose problems pertaining to the supporter's own life which may add to the concerns of the other, or to benefit from their knowledge or expertise in any way. Using counselling skills can generate a relationship in which the individual can be unduly grateful for the attention and efforts proffered them. Professionals who have insight into their own personal motivations and drives in the job can generally retain a sense of perspective on the relationship.

The professional and effective use of counselling skills engenders a situation in which supporters are afforded a power which they would not otherwise have. They are dealing with individuals who are temporarily vulnerable and who may desire or need sustained support. Acting in a way which is congruent with a counselling relationship, and clearly maintaining boundaries, can provide a safe and containing relationship for the duration of the interaction. Caution has to be exercised prior to engaging in any relationship beyond that of the formal supporting relationship. Inclinations to extend or transform a relationship may reflect the supporter's own neediness or vulnerability at the time. It can be helpful to remember that situations which entail a high degree of physiological arousal and adrenalin and which may also be life threatening, as in the case of traumatic incidents, can serve to intensify emotions of closeness. Such emotions are often transient and peculiar to the circumstances. Those proffering support should be aware of their own heightened feelings and those of others at such times; this helps to maintain a perspective on the situation (Gutheil and Gabbard 1993). In accordance with professional codes of ethics, any change in the professional relationship should involve consultation with a supervisor or manager. If professionals enter into a relationship which affords sexual gratification or financial or material gain as a result of the use of counselling skills, then it would be considered an exploitation of their professional role.

Depending on the particular profession within the emergency services, helping an individual may involve varying degrees of *touch* from comfort to medical intervention. Using touch in combination with counselling skills is a little researched area and often controversial (Hetherington 1998; Hunter and Struve 1998). While touch can have beneficial effects under certain circumstances, it can also intensify the intimacy of the interaction, particularly in conjunction with counselling skills. Nonmedical touch for the purpose of comfort and support may be much welcomed and appreciated by individuals feeling emotional and needy. Yet for some individuals who may have experienced childhood abuse, touch may be associated with feelings of fear and distress. In a profession in which touch is often necessary, it is important for supporters to have a good knowledge of the effects of touch both on their own feelings and those of others, and to exercise appropriate ethical constraints in its use.

All these considerations entail supporters being self-aware and monitoring changes in their own outlook, motivations and needs. A vulnerable individual, grateful for the support and attention offered to them, can have a very distorted view of both the supporter's role and their nature. This can feel very welcome to supporters who are experiencing their own problems and for personal reasons temporarily feeling unappreciated. Being aware of these kinds of personal feelings and of the circumstances in which they arise is important to protect both the individual and the supporter's vulnerability.

For professionals fulfilling a supporting role, it is very easy to believe that they can and must cope. The accumulation of coping with their own difficulties and those of others will incur an effect. It is important again here to recognize this and to seek and accept support from others when necessary. In accordance with the BAC code of practice, an individual should not attempt to employ counselling skills with others when their 'functioning is impaired due to personal or emotional difficulties, illness, disability, alcohol, drugs or for any other reason' (British Association of Counselling 1998: B2.18).

Case: changing relationships

Marilyn was involved in an industrial accident and assisted at the scene by a paramedic, Fred. Fred immediately related to Marilyn, who bore a considerable similarity to his ex-wife. He later checked on her recovery in hospital, and provided emotional support. Marilyn was grateful to Fred for all his help. He asked if he could call to see her at home. Given the marked age difference, Marilyn assumed that Fred was acting in a professional and paternal manner. However, Fred would not normally provide professional support beyond the immediate incident. He had assumed that he was relating to Marilyn outside of his professional role. He felt that this was verified by Marilyn allowing him to visit her at home. On the evening he called to see her, he touched her hands and face and expressed how much he liked her. Marilyn did not react until after he had left, when she felt overcome by fear. She felt responsible, and that she must have misled him. She made every effort to avoid him. He continued to call, concerned for her well-being. Finally, in a state of distress, she lodged a complaint against him.

In this illustration, Marilyn's sense of gratitude, vulnerability and trust of Fred as a professional was misconstrued by Fred and potentially exploited. Marilyn had experienced Fred only in his professional capacity. However, Fred perceived that his professional role had ended once she was in hospital care. In Marilyn's similarity to his wife, he imbued her with a feeling of familiarity. However, any extension of the relationship outside of Fred's capacity as an emergency service professional was incongruent with Marilyn's perception of Fred. Marilyn was responding to his professional role with its inherent status and power, not to him as an individual. When Fred transformed the relationship, Marilyn felt helpless in restoring the balance of power. Her appreciation of his role in her recovery prevented her reacting appropriately. Both parties needed a third independent body to resolve the issue and to ensure that Fred's personal need for support was appropriately addressed before resuming a counselling skills role. The complaint enabled the employing organization to refine its own policy with regard to the nature of a professional relationship and the use of counselling skills.

Value judgements in the use of counselling skills

For the professional using counselling skills, it is essential to be aware of personal values, judgements and prejudice. For those working with law and order, the discrepancy between the values they hold and the public with whom they interact may at times be considerable. Similar incompatibility in values may arise in the medical profession in relation to some individuals who are being treated. On occasions where differences in attitudes are irreconcilable, it may be appropriate to state the difference. Verbalizing differences in views at such times may model the appropriate management of conflict. In such instances, active use of counselling skills may feel incongruent, lacking the genuineness necessary to be effective, but the opportunity to express differences verbally need not prevent relating and proffering help to the individual. However, in using counselling skills in the workplace with colleagues, prejudiced attitudes tend to interfere with the value of any support provided.

Individuals, particularly at times of vulnerability, easily detect inferred or repressed criticism. At the same time, many of the difficulties encountered by employees may emanate from prejudice and ill-informed views. An awareness of the societal origins of prejudice and the psychological nature of 'scapegoating' is essential in the practice of counselling skills (see Douglas 1995).

In the course of using counselling skills with peers or with the public, individuals are required to adhere not only to the BAC code of ethics in relation to anti-discriminatory practice, but also to their employer's own equal opportunities policy in regard to sex, race and disability. Actions involving sexual harassment can be brought under the Sex Discrimination Act 1975.

In addition, the Department of Employment (1995) recommends that an organization has clear policies in the event of sexual harassment in the workplace, accompanied by a comprehensive complaints procedure. Individuals who experience discrimination in the workplace may need to be informed of the appropriate course of action for them to take (see Thomas and Kitzinger 1997 for further discussion).

Complaints and grievances procedures

An organization that promotes training in and effective use of counselling skills should also provide information on a systematic complaints procedure, in accordance with professional ethical requirements. This serves to allow organizations to monitor and maintain the standard and quality of their employees' use of professional skills. It also allows claims of malpractice to be addressed and resolved. Where an organization or an individual is a member of a professional body such as BAC or UKCP (United Kingdom Council for Psychotherapy), complaints may be made to the appropriate organization and will be processed according to their specific policies. Information on complaints procedures should be readily available within the organization. The relationship between professional standards and complaints is inextricably woven, as Palmer Barnes (1998) suggests:

> Concern about how to manage complaints has in its turn led to a tightening up of ethical standards and guidelines for codes of conduct. The clarification of these codes and boundaries is in itself very helpful in the processing of complaints. A proper understanding of ethical issues and careful managing of complaints are also seen as essential factors in maintaining standards and establishing good practice within a profession.
>
> (Palmer Barnes 1998: 2)

Complaints may serve a useful purpose in highlighting consumer awareness and ensuring high standards of professional practice. Moreover, they also bear potential legal implications. A just and effective complaints procedure may serve to reduce the threat of legal action against the employing organization. Conversely, a complaint not satisfactorily resolved can be pursued to resolution through the courts. Recent government initiatives on promoting consumer rights and implementing accessible complaints procedures through the network of citizen's charters have enabled complainants to seek redress in a wide range of situations (HMG 1991).

Fundamental principles

For the individual reporting inappropriate professional practice, the response they receive through the complaints procedure is crucial to their view of the organization, and will influence their attitudes about the core elements of trust, respect and high standards of practice embodied in the professional relationship (Jenkins 1997). For this reason the organizational complaints procedure must embrace the principles of good practice. Some of the key elements to be considered in any complaints system include issues of advocacy, lay representation, the role of natural justice and overall responsiveness to client needs. The Wilson Report on complaints systems in the NHS advocates a number of fundamental principles underpinning an effective and responsive procedure (Department of Health 1994: 30). They include:

- offering an apology, while not necessarily accepting legal responsibility for the cause of the complaint
- providing a speedy acknowledgement and response to the complaint
- giving the individual a firm assurance that the complaint is being taken seriously, and that measures have been introduced to prevent it recurring.

Natural justice

All complaints systems should take account both of the interests of the consumer and of those of the provider. Complaints systems which disregard the fundamental principles of natural justice are liable to legal challenge. In an effort to ensure fairness, a balance must be struck between preserving a degree of informality which encourages client access and resolution of complaints, while conducting sufficiently formal a procedure to protect the rights of all involved. To this end, investigation into the complaint must apply fundamental principles of justice which entail that (Jakobi 1995):

- the individual, against whom the complaint is made, is informed of the complaint and permitted to respond in person
- no person directly involved in the complaint should sit in judgement of the case
- both parties involved in the complaint are allowed to present their view of events
- all parties should have access to any material such as documents and records which are relevant to the case.

Advocacy and lay representation

Where individuals lodging a complaint are considered to be in a position of relative powerlessness, professional bodies may be available who can provide the appropriate support to empower them. The Wilson Report points to the potential role of advocacy in supporting complainants (Department of Health 1994: 44). Having access to advocacy and lay representation could help individuals who feel disadvantaged in making a complaint against a seemingly powerful organization (Hansen 1994). Any body fulfilling such a role is required to be familiar with the complex professional issues involved. In general, such procedures can ensure that all grievances against an organization are resolved rather than sustained, and that professional standards are promoted and maintained.

Individuals can experience a number of difficulties in lodging a complaint against a professional, such as language barriers, disclosure of professional abuse, or the perception of the individual versus the organization. For these reasons, complaints procedures need to model a process of empowerment for the individual, while reflecting the growing culture of consumer rights in the service and training sectors. Complaints to either professional associations or to independent organizational bodies can be an effective option for dissatisfied individuals in achieving a satisfactory outcome and wherever possible retaining the individual's goodwill.

The combination of legal, statutory and professional standards of practice reflect both the value placed on the competent use of counselling skills and their potential to do damage.

It is incumbent on both professionals employing counselling skills and the employing organization to be fully familiar with legal and ethical issues. Anticipation of any potential problems and a knowledge of appropriate procedures for their resolution is central to the safe and productive use of counselling skills in the workplace.

Further reading

Bond, T. (2000) *Standards and Ethics for Counselling in Action*, 2nd edn. London: Sage.

Clarkson, P. (1997) *The Bystander: An End to Innocence in Human Relationships?* London: Whurr.

Douglas, T. (1995) *Scapegoats: Transferring Blame*. London: Routledge.

Hunter, M. and Struve, J. (1998) *The Ethical Use of Touch in Psychotherapy*. London: Sage.

Jenkins, P. (1997) *Counselling, Psychotherapy and the Law*. London: Sage.

Palmer Barnes, F. (1998) *Complaints and Grievances in Psychotherapy: A Handbook of Ethical Practice*. London: Routledge.

Pederson, P.B. (2000) *Hidden Messages in Culture-Centred Counselling: A Triad Training Model*. London: Sage.

Walker, M. (1990) *Women in Therapy and Counselling*. Buckingham: Open University Press.

Chapter **8**

Conclusion

Emergency service professionals employ counselling skills on a daily basis to enable them to manage people who are in a distressed or disturbed state as a result of crime, accident, illness, or injury to themselves or others. To be effective requires fundamental interpersonal attributes of empathy, congruousness and genuineness forged with refined listening and attending skills. These core competencies are developed through a sound knowledge base coupled with a constant re-evaluation and moderation of personal behaviour in situations requiring counselling skills. With increasing experience, the use of counselling skills becomes a highly developed form of communication for use with individuals in emergency situations. Moreover, the trained use of counselling skills is frequently instrumental to the achievement of the professional's primary objectives.

Given the nature of emergency service work, counselling skills are predominantly used in responding to people involved in critical and traumatic incidents. This requires the professional to have a sound working knowledge of the immediate and delayed effects of post traumatic stress. However, responding appropriately to traumatic events, founded on a thorough understanding of the nature of traumatic stress, is significantly enhanced by ongoing supervised experience. Controlled experience on the job, together with working as part of a fully functioning team, is integral to the competent application of counselling skills in the field.

Emergency service workers are also subject to the cumulative and adverse effects of frequent exposure to traumatic events. This requires professionals to exercise an active responsibility for their own psychological well-being, remaining sensitive to the personal impact of frequent and systematic exposure to traumatic incidents (Gist and Woodall 1995). An intrinsic aspect of the professional's success is their ability to recognize their personal needs for ongoing support, supervision and continuing professional development from their employing organization. Initiating and accessing appropriate support when necessary is frequently a significant indicator of the professional's personal competence in employing support skills effectively with others.

Counselling skills are equally valuable when applied in a controlled context within the organization with fellow workers. This usually takes the form of a trained peer support programme. In this context, the systematic use of counselling skills are further enhanced by the emergency service worker's personal experience of the occupational environment and an understanding of the nature of the job. For personnel experiencing work place difficulties, there is a natural affinity towards others who have undergone similar experiences. Tapping and developing this natural support structure can moderate the impact of occupational stress on employees. It can also serve to promote a healthy and productive working environment.

While peer support programmes can increase the accessibility of support, it is integral to their success that they are operated with an explicit knowledge of their limitations. They remain pivotal in providing an immediate source of support and well informed resource for referral. Where specialist professional interventions are necessary, however, peer support is not intended as a substitute. The successful development of a formal peer support programme within an emergency service must be founded on a clearly defined organizational recruitment, selection, supervision and evaluation policy. The peer support programme and the peer supporters must be supervised by mental health professionals. This is most usually provided through internal occupational health and welfare departments, external employee assistance programmes or most effectively a combination of the two (Berridge *et al.* 1997).

It is through proactive organizational strategies such as a comprehensive employee assistance programme that the organization actively exercises a 'duty of care' to employees, limiting the potentially pernicious effects of frequent exposure to traumatic incidents. An integral component of a successful employee assistance programme is the regular training of employees in the effects and normality of occupational and traumatic stress. Providing a standard occupational and traumatic stress awareness programme also serves to promote an organizational culture which destigmatizes the need for support (Catherall 1995). Undoubtedly, providing timely and focused support to employees can be mutually beneficial to both the organization and the individual in maintaining personal performance, productivity, job satisfaction, commitment and general psychological well-being (Philips *et al.* 1997).

The professional use of counselling skills within the emergency service environment can have a marked positive effect on the individuals with whom they are used. However, if an intervention has the power to do good it can equally hold the potential to do damage. Just as medication administered by trained practitioners can promote recovery, used inappropriately it can potentially incur serious and devastating consequences. Increasingly research points to the adverse effects of uncontrolled interventions, particularly in the event of trauma (Tehrani 1998). For this reason it is essential that counselling skills are practised in the full knowledge of their clinical and legal limitations. Professional codes of practice in clearly defining the parameters to the use of counselling skills provide safety and assurance to the public, the professional and to the organization. It falls to both the individual emergency service professional and to their employing organization to ensure that they are clearly practised.

Emergency service professionals work primarily with traumatic events, managing not only the situation but also the people involved in them. Their main tool in doing so is often the power of their personality, their skills and their training rather than the authority of their role. Having first hand experience of frequent exposure to traumatic events gives them an insight, empathy and competency which frequently eludes others in supporting roles. Yet such experience, even with a knowledge of the subject, is impotent without the skills necessary to utilize them. Counselling skills provide the medium through which knowledge and experience are employed to manage people in a full range of often complex and sometimes catastrophic life events. Ultimately, the trained use of counselling skills serves to enhance the effectiveness and competency of emergency professionals in doing their jobs.

Appendix **A**

Symptoms of post traumatic stress disorder

Post traumatic stress is a normal reaction to an abnormal event. It inter-feres with normal feelings and behaviour. Reactions usually persist for around four weeks, but may take longer to abate. Sometimes, reactions to the event may be delayed. Often current traumatic incidents 'trigger' feelings towards previous traumatic events, compounding the individu-al's reactions to the current trauma. Traumatic stressors can potentially have a prolonged effect on personality, patterns of adjustment, coping styles and interpersonal functioning.

Post traumatic stress is a dynamic survivor syndrome. It has ele-ments of many known psychiatric disorders but is a unique syndrome of adjustment to traumatic events.

Dimensions of personality affected by delayed stress reaction

Physiological and emotional responses

These kinds of responses include:

- feelings of detachment or numbness
- reduced range of affect and unresponsiveness to others
- loss of interest in work and personal activities, fatigue, lethargy
- avoidance of activities that arouse memories or resemble the trau-matic event
- hyper-alertness, startle easily, irritability
- hyper-vigilant of surroundings and impending danger

- loss of sense of invulnerability, and sense of foreshortened future
- sleep disturbances and recurring nightmares of the trauma
- 'flashbacks' and acting or feeling as if the event was recurring
- intense distress in response to triggers symbolic of the trauma
- depression: helplessness, apathy, dejection, sadness, isolation
- anger, rage, resentment, hostility (feeling like a 'walking time-bomb')
- anxiety and specific fears associated with the traumatic experience
- suicidal feelings and thoughts; self-destructive behavioural tendencies
- tendency to react under stress with 'survival tactics'
- intensification of 'normal developmental growth crises'
- sense of shame and guilt over circumstances or symptoms
- survivor guilt
- reduced sex drive.

Cognitive responses

Examples of cognitive responses include:

- difficulty concentrating
- recycling thoughts of the traumatic incident
- fantasies of retaliation and destruction, changes in attitudes and value system
- cynicism and distrust of authority and the criminal justice system
- alienation: feeling like an outsider; life seems meaninglessness
- negative self-image, low self-esteem
- memory impairment
- hyper-sensitivity to issues of equity, justice, fairness, equality and legitimacy.

Interpersonal relationships

The effects on relationships can include:

- problems in establishing or maintaining intimate relationships
- tendency to have difficulties with authoritative figures (challenging and testing authority, rules and regulations)
- emotional distance from children and significant others
- concern about anger alienating children, spouse and others
- self-deceiving and self-punishing patterns of relating
- inability to talk about the traumatic experiences and feelings
- tendency to explode in fits of rage and anger; especially with use of alcohol or drugs.

Appendix B

Secondary symptoms of post traumatic stress disorder

Various additional symptoms to those listed in DSM IV have been noted in individuals manifesting PTSD. They are included here for the purpose of facilitating a more complete understanding of PTSD and assisting in the recognition of PTSD where primary symptoms are not evident, but where there may be reason to believe that the individual's problems originate from the experience of a traumatic event.

The more frequently reported secondary symptoms of PTSD are depression, anxiety, death imprint/anxiety, impulsive behaviour, substance abuse, somatization/tension, alterations in time sense and character changes.

Depression

This may include a high percentage of the following depressive features:

- feeling low in energy or slowed down
- crying easily
- overwhelming sadness
- losing interest in life
- feeling hopeless about the future
- feelings of worthlessness
- loss of sexual interest or pleasure
- generalized fatigue
- recurrent depressive feelings and suicidal thoughts.

Anxiety

A number of the following features of anxiety would be evident:

- generalized anxiety
- panic disorders
- feeling tense
- nervousness/edginess
- feeling fearful
- sudden unprovoked fear
- heart palpitations
- hyperventilation
- excessive sweating.

Death imprint/death anxiety

'Death imprint' and 'death anxiety' are important features in survivors of severe traumatization, who may have experienced death and destruction on a large scale. Symptoms include:

- a feeling of threat
- a feeling of imminent death
- fear of recurrence of trauma – intrusive images of death
- loss of sense of invulnerability.

Impulsive behaviour

In addition to the symptoms described in DSM IV, impulsive behaviour may also take the form of:

- sudden unaccountable trips
- unexplained absences
- changes in lifestyle or residence.

Substance abuse

Self-medication with alcohol can, in the first instance, be effective in suppressing the symptoms of PTSD. It can assist in inducing sleep, reducing anxiety, preventing disturbing dreams and easing muscle tension. With time, however, its effect diminishes and it may serve to exacerbate the symptoms. The development of alcoholism frequently occurs in addition to classic PTSD symptomology.

Somatization/tension

A broad range of physical symptoms may be reported in individuals suffering from PTSD. These may include feelings of exhaustion, feelings of weakness, excessive tension, headaches, muscle pains, allergenic symptoms, ulcers, colitis, gastric overactivity, respiratory or cardiac syndromes, hypochondriasis.

Alterations in time sense

Alterations in time sense do not occur with the same frequency as other PTSD symptoms but may still be indicative of traumatic stress in the absence of other symptoms. Time distortions may affect the recollection of the traumatic incident in the following ways:

- speeding up or slowing down of time
- confusion over time sequence of events
- events occurring during the trauma are placed prior to it – retrospectively formed 'warnings' of event
- a sense of dreams being predicative, allowing individuals psychic abilities.

Character changes

A number of character changes have been noted in relation to PTSD particularly in those exposed to large scale disasters. They include:

- excessive defensiveness
- regression
- rigid defensiveness/fragility of defensiveness under stress
- reduced personal resources
- hostility
- withdrawal from challenges
- negative decline in character and in management of effects.

Miscellaneous secondary features

Other symptoms of PTSD may be general adjustment problems, long term interactional problems, sexual difficulties, feelings of mistrust, feelings of betrayal, feelings of being scapegoated and negative self-image. A percentage of individuals suffering from PTSD may display a number of additional symptoms. These symptoms may be evident in the apparent absence of primary symptoms. However, an individual need not exhibit secondary symptoms to be considered to be suffering from PTSD.

Appendix C

Symptoms of stress

The effects of stress are most easily detectable by *changes* in behaviour. The greater the number or intensity of changes, the greater the extent of disruption to the individual's life. Stress is a normal and common response, which, with appropriate action, will subside. Responding to early signs of stress may mitigate the cumulative and severe stress reactions which may otherwise be experienced by the individual.

Signs of stress

Signs of stress may be found across a range of behavioural, physical, emotional and cognitive areas, as listed below.

Behavioural signs

Drug abuse, excessive smoking or drinking, change in activity level, withdrawal, suspiciousness, change in interpersonal behaviour, increased concern over environment, excessive humour, inappropriate behaviour.

Physical signs

Tremors of lips and fingers, nausea, upset stomach, excess sweating, feeling cold, rapid heart beat, poor sleep, dry mouth, general fatigue, trembling.

Emotional signs

Generalized anxiety, excessive fear, survivor guilt, depression, increased emotionality, feelings of futility, feeling isolated, feeling numb, unable to communicate, anger.

Cognitive signs

Inability to concentrate, difficulty remembering, confusion, low attention capacity, calculation problems, intrusive thoughts, disturbing dreams.

Significant symptoms of stress

Certain symptoms of stress require immediate medical attention. These are listed below.

Behavioural symptoms

Change in speech patterns, uncontrolled anger or crying, extreme hyperactivity.

Physical symptoms

Chest pains, difficulties in breathing, cardiac arrhythmias, collapse from exhaustion, symptoms of severe shock, dizziness.

Emotional symptoms

Panic or phobic reactions, shock-like state, inappropriate reactions.

Cognitive symptoms

Unresponsive to surroundings, indecisive, hyper-alert, general mental confusion, disorientation, impaired thinking, problems recognizing familiar items or people.

These stress indicators are not exhaustive. Stress may manifest itself in a variety of forms. For more detailed information on the physiological effects of stress see Toates (1995).

Reactions to stress

Reactions to stress may be delayed, occurring days or weeks after a stressful event, rendering the reactions all the more confusing as they are not immediately associated with the event. Similarly, stress reactions need not be a response to one extreme incident but may occur as a result of prolonged exposure to stressors. This can result in prolonged stress duress syndrome (PSDS), in which the individual experiences a similar set of characteristic reactions to that of PTSD.

Appendix D

Referral resources

For emergency service employees who need specialist professional support, it is important to have a pre-established network of suitable referral resources. Frequently mental health professionals know little of the reality of emergency service work, and equally emergency service personnel may be unfamiliar with the role of a mental health specialist. Myths and false expectations can create obstacles when the need for help and support arises. Identifying mental health professionals who have experience of PTSD and the emergency service environment and culture will help in breaking down communication barriers.

Clinical and occupational psychologists

The most likely person to be employed in this capacity is either a clinical or occupational psychologist, both of whom by their title will hold a postgraduate qualification in their area of specialization. A clinical psychologist may assist in determining individual psychological problems and their subsequent treatment. An occupational psychologist is qualified to identify and assist in work-related, individual or organizational problems. These psychologists will also be qualified in administering and interpreting diagnostic psychological tests, as appropriate to their field of specialization. Experience in disaster or trauma psychology would be of particular importance in the event of critical incident debriefing.

Counsellors

A counsellor would normally be accredited with a professional body, which may be the British Association of Counselling or the British Psychological Society (BPS). Each of these professional bodies specifies the qualifications, training and supervised experience deemed necessary for professional practice and ensures that all accredited counsellors comply with these standards. Professional counsellors would hold an MSc in counselling, or a recognized postgraduate diploma in counselling or professional accreditation.

Social workers

Social workers often hold a postgraduate qualification, and usually work within hospitals, mental health centres and clinics. They mostly specialize in family and group problems, and are usually experienced in bereavement, and often in trauma counselling within family groups.

Psychiatric nurses

Psychiatric nurses often hold a postgraduate qualification and work mostly in a hospital or clinical setting. Although normally working with severely disturbed people, many psychiatric nurses also work within a private practice and may specialize in post traumatic stress disorder.

Psychiatrists

Psychiatrists are medical doctors who are qualified to prescribe medication and to conduct other medical tasks in the treatment of psychological problems. They would usually deal with mental disturbances of a more persistent or severe nature. Disaster and trauma psychiatry is a growing area of specialization within this profession. It will take time for a person to feel comfortable and confident with the choice of counsellor. The professional's capacity to help will ultimately depend upon the individual's ability to be open and honest in discussions with the professional and committed to counselling.

Referrals to a specialist

Confidential referral to a specialist can be via the peer supporter to the welfare department or employee assistance provider. Internal welfare departments will employ counsellors in-house and specialists on a fee-for-service basis. External employee assistance providers will normally employ counsellors and psychologists, and use psychiatrists on a consultancy basis. However, emergency professionals may prefer to self-refer to a specialist in work-related trauma. For this reason, the names of suitable professionals should be openly available in the workplace. Both the BPS and the BAC provide directories of professionals.

Bibliography

Alexander, D.A. (1993) Stress among police body handlers: a long-term follow up, *British Journal of Psychiatry*, 163: 806–8.

American Psychiatric Association (APA) (1994) *Diagnostic and Statistical Manual of Mental Disorders*, 4th edn (DSM IV). Washington, DC: APA.

Argyris, C. and Schon, D. (1984) What is an organisation that it may learn, in B. Paton, S. Brown, R. Spear *et al.* (eds) *Organisations*. London: Paul Chapman.

Arroba, T. and James, K. (1988) Police: interrogators into counsellors, *Occupational Psychologist*, 6 December.

Beaton, R., Murphy, S., Johnson, C., Pike, K. and Corneil, W. (1998) Exposure to duty-related incident stressors in urban firefighters and paramedics, *Journal of Traumatic Stress*, 11(4): 821–8.

Beaton, R., Murphy, S., Johnson, C., Pike, K. and Corneil, W. (1999) Coping responses and post traumatic stress symptomology in urban fire service personnel, *Journal of Traumatic Stress*, 12(2): 293–308.

Berridge, J., Cooper, C. and Highley-Marchington, C. (1997) *Employee Assistance Programmes and Workplace Counselling*. Chichester: Wiley.

Bond, T. (1992) Confidentiality: counselling, ethics and the law, *Employee Counselling Today*, 4(4): 4–9.

Bond, T. (1999) Confidentiality, counselling and the law, *Counselling at Work*, 26.

Bond, T. (2000) *Standards and Ethics for Counselling in Action*, 2nd edn. London: Sage.

Bor, R., Miller, R., Latz, M. and Sait, H. (1998) *Counselling in Health Care Settings*. London: Massell.

Bradbury, A. (1993) Therapists and data protection, *The Therapist*, 1(1): 4.

British Association for Sexual and Marital Therapy (BASMT) (1991) *Code of Practice*. Sheffield: BASMT.

British Association of Counselling (BAC) (1989) *Code of Ethics and Practice for Counselling Skills*. Rugby: BAC.

British Association of Counselling (1998) *Guidelines for Those Using Counselling Skills in their Work*. Rugby: BAC.

British Association of Counselling (1999) *Confidentiality, Counselling and the Law*. Rugby: BAC.

British Association of Social Workers (BASW) (1995) *Case book, Professional Social Work*, 7–8 January.

Bryant, R. and Harvey, A. (1996) Post traumatic stress reaction in volunteer firefighters, *Journal of Traumatic Stress*, 9: 51–2.

Carkhuff, R.R. (1987) *The Art of Helping*, 6th edn. Amherst, MA: Human Resource Development Press.

Carroll, M. (1994) Making ethical decisions in organisational counselling, *EAP International*, 1(4): 26–30.

Carroll, M. (1995) The counsellor in organisational settings: some reflections, *Employee Counselling Today*, 7(1): 23–9.

Carroll, M. (1996) *Workplace Counselling: A Systematic Approach to Employee Care*. London: Sage.

Carroll, M. and Walton, M. (eds) (1997) *Handbook of Counselling in Organisations*. London: Sage.

Catherall, D. (1995) Preventing institutional secondary traumatic stress disorder, in C. Figley (ed.) *Compassion Fatigue: Coping with Secondary Traumatic Stress Disorder in Those Who Treat the Traumatised*. New York: Brunner Mazel.

Clarkson, P. (1997) *The Bystander: An End to Innocence in Human Relationships?* London: Whurr.

Cooper, C. (1995) The worrier mentality, *Management Today*, January: 14.

Corneil, W. (1995) Traumatic stress and organisational strain in the fire service, in L. Murphy, J. Hurrell, J.R. Sauter and G. Keiter (eds) *Job Stress Interventions*. Washington, DC: APA Press.

Covey, S.R. (1989) *The Seven Habits of Highly Effective People*. New York: Simon and Schuster.

Davis, M.H. (1996) *Empathy: A Social Psychological Approach*. Oxford: Westview Press.

Department of Employment (DE) (1995) *How Equal Opportunities Can Benefit Your Business*. London: DE.

Department of Health (DoH) (1994) *Being Heard: The Report of a Review Committee on NHS Complaints Procedures* (Wilson Report). London: DoH.

Douglas, T. (1995) *Scapegoats: Transferring Blame*. London: Routledge.

Duan, C. and Hill, C.E. (1996) The current state of empathy research, *Journal of Counselling Psychology*, 43(3): 261–74.

Duckworth, D.H. (1991) Everyday psychological trauma in the police service, *Disaster Management*, 3(4).

Dyregrov, A. (1989) Caring for helpers in disaster situations: psychological debriefing, *Disaster Management*, 2: 25–30.

Dutfield, M. and Ealing, C. (1990) *The Communicating Manager*. Shaftesbury: Element Books.

Earnshaw, J.M. and Cooper, C.L. (1996) *Stress and Employer Liability*. London: Institute of Personnel and Development.

Edwards, C.E. and Murdock, N.L. (1994) Characteristics of therapist self-disclosure in the counselling process, *Journal of Counselling and Development*, 72: 384–9.

Egan, G. (1986) *The Skilled Helper: A Systematic Approach to Effective Helping*, 3rd edn. Belmont, CA: Brooks/Cole.

Egan, G. (1998) *The Skilled Helper: A Problem-Management Approach to Helping*, 6th edn. Pacific Grove, CA: Brooks/Cole.

Einzig, H. and Evans, R. (1990) *Personal Problems at Work: Counselling as a Resource for the Manager*. Rugby: British Association for Counselling.

Ekman, P. (1992) *Telling Lies: Clues to Deceit in the Market Place, Politics, and Marriage*. New York: Norton.

Employee Assistance Programmes Association (EAPA) (1995) *UK Standards of Practice and Professional Guidelines for Employee Assistance Programmes*. London: EAPA.

Eysenck, H.J. (1994) The outcome problem in psychotherapy: what have we learned, *Behavior Research and Therapy*, 32(5): 477–95.

Feldman, D. (1985) Access to clients' documents after the Police and Criminal Act, *Professional Negligence*, January/February: 24–9, March/April: 67–72.

Feltham, C. (1997) *The Gains of Listening: Perspectives on Counselling at Work*. Buckingham: Open University Press.

Figley, C. (ed.) (1994) *Trauma and its Wake*. New York: Brunner Mazel.

Figley, C. (ed.) (1995) *Compassion Fatigue: Coping with Secondary Traumatic Stress Disorder in Those who Treat the Traumatised*. New York: Brunner Mazel.

Fitzpatrick, J. (1994) in T. Ravenscroft, Conference reports, traumatic stress and the emergency services, *Disaster Management*, 6(1).

Follette, V.M., Polusny, M.M. and Milbeck, K. (1994) Mental health and law enforcement professionals: traumatic history, psychological symptoms, and impact of providing services to child sexual abuse survivors, *Professional Psychology: Research and Practice*, 25(3): 275–82.

Follette, V.M., Ruzek, J. and Abueg, F. (1998) *Cognitive Behavioural Therapies for Trauma*. New York: Guilford Press.

Fowler, A. (1991) How to provide employee counselling, *Personnel Management Plus*, May: 24–5.

Gist, R. and Woodall, S.J. (1995) Occupational stress in contemporary fire service, *Occupational Medicine: State of the Art Reviews*, 10(4): 763–87.

Goodyear, R.K. and Shumate, J.L. (1996) Perceived effects of therapist self-disclosure of attraction to clients, *Professional Psychology: Research and Practice*, 27(6): 613–16.

Grigsby, D.Y. and McKnew, M.A. (1988) Work-stress burnout amongst paramedics, *Psychological Reports*, 63: 55–64.

Grosch, W.N. and Olsen, D.C. (1994) *Where Helping Starts to Hurt*. London: Norton.

Gutheil, T.G. and Gabbard, G.O. (1993) The concept of boundaries in clinical practice: theoretical and risk-management dimensions, *American Journal of Psychiatry*, 150(2): 188–96.

Halleck, S.L. (1988) Which patients are responsible for their illnesses, *American Journal of Psychotherapy*, 42: 338–53.

Hansen, O. (1994) *The Solicitors Complaints Bureau: A Consumer View*. London: National Consumer Council.

Hattie, J.A., Sharpley, C.E. and Rogers, H.J. (1984) Comparative effectiveness of professional and paraprofessional helpers, *Psychological Bulletin*, 95: 534–41.

Hawkins, P. and Shohet, R. (2000) *Supervision in the Helping Professions*. Buckingham: Open University Press.

Health and Safety Commission (HSC) (1992) *Management of Health and Safety at Work: Health and Safety Regulations 1992*. London: HSC.

Health and Safety Executive (HSE) (1995) *Health and Safety at Work, 1995: The Act Outlined*. London: HSE.

Herman, J.L. (1992) *Trauma and Recovery: From Domestic Abuses to Political Terror*. London: HarperCollins.

Her Majesty's Government (AMG) (1991) *Citizens' Charters*, Cm 1599. London: HMSO.

Hetherington, A. (1992) *The Extent and Source of Stress in the Emergency Service*. Report no. 9110. Cranfield: Cranfield Institute.

Hetherington, A. (1993) *Human Resource Management in Times of Stress*. Police Research Group. London: The Home Office.

Hetherington, A. (1998) The use and abuse of touch in therapy and counselling, *Counselling Psychology Quarterly*, 11: 361–4.

Hetherington, A. (2000) Exploitation in therapy and counselling: a breach of professional standards, *British Journal of Guidance and Counselling*, 28: 11–22.

Hetherington, A. and Munro, A. (1997) At the scene: road accidents and the police, in M. Mitchell (ed.) *The Aftermath of Road Accidents: The Psychological, Social and Legal Consequences of an Everyday Trauma*. London: Routledge.

Hewitt, P. (1993) *About Time: The Revolution in Family Life*. London: Rivers Oram.

Higgins, E.T. (1987) Self-discrepancy: a theory relating self and affect, *Psychological Review*, 94: 319–40.

Hill, C.E., Thompson, B.G., Cogar, M.C. and Denmann III, D.W. (1993) Beneath the surface of long-term therapy: therapist and client reports of their own and each others' covert processes, *Journal of Counselling Psychology*, 40(3): 278–87.

Hodgkinson, P.E. and Stewart, M. (1991) *Coping with Catastrophe*. London: Routledge.

Hodgkinson, P.E., Joseph, S., Yule, W. and Williams, R. (1993) Viewing human remains following disaster: helpful or harmful? *Medicine, Science and the Law*, 33: 197–202.

Hoffman, M.L. (1987) The contribution of empathy to justice and moral judgement, in N. Eisenberg and J. Strayer (eds) *Empathy and its Development*. Cambridge: Cambridge University Press.

Holmes, J. and Lindley, R. (1994) Ethics and psychotherapy, in R. Gillon (ed.) *Principles of Health Care Ethics*. Chichester: Wiley.

Horowitz, M.J. (1978) *Stress Response Syndromes*. New York: Jason Aronson.

Hough, M. (1998) *Counselling Skills and Theory*. London: Hodder and Stoughton.

Hughes, J.M. (1991) *Counselling for Managers: An Introductory Guide*. London: Bacie.

Hunter, M. and Struve, J. (1998) *The Ethical Use of Touch in Therapy*. London: Sage.

Hunter, R.H. (1995) Benefits of competency-based treatment programs, *American Psychologist*, 50: 509–13.

Institute for Personnel Development (IPD) (1995) *Guide on Employee Data*. London: IPD.

Jacobs, M. (1998) *The Presenting Past*, 2nd edn. Buckingham: Open University Press.

Jacobs, M. (1999) *Psychodynamic Counselling in Action*, 2nd edn. London: Sage.

Jakobi, S. (1995) *The Law and the Training of Counsellors and Psychotherapists*. London: Royal Society of Medicine.

James, A. (1988) Perceptions of stress in British ambulance personnel, *Work and Stress*, 2(4): 319–26.

Jarvie, D. and Matthews, J. (1989) A counselling approach to development management, *Training and Development*, August: 9–10.

Jenkins, P. (1997) *Counselling, Psychotherapy and the Law*. London: Sage.

Jones, C., Shillito-Clarke, C., Syme, G., Hill, D. and Casemore, R. (2000) *Questions of Ethics in Counselling and Therapy*. Buckingham: Open University Press.

Joseph, S., Williams, R. and Yule, W. (1993) Changes in outlook following disaster, *Journal of Traumatic Stress*, 6: 271–9.

Joseph, S., Williams, R. and Yule, W. (1997) *Understanding Post Traumatic Stress: A Psychosocial Perspective on PTSD and Treatment*. Chichester: Wiley.

Knapp, M.L. (1978) *Nonverbal Communication in Human Interaction*, 2nd edn. New York: Holt, Rinehart and Winston.

Kristofferson, J.I. (1990) Psychological debriefing with police officers. Paper presented at the Second Conference on Traumatic Stress. Utrecht, Netherlands.

Lago, C. (1996) *Race, Culture and Counselling*. Buckingham: Open University Press.

Luborsky, L. (1993) The promise of new psychosocial treatments or the inability of non-significant differences – a poll of the experts, *Psychotherapy and Rehabilitation Research Bulletin*, 2: 6–8.

McCammon, S. (1996) Emergency medical service worker: occupational stress and traumatic stress, in D. Paton and J. Violanti (eds) *Traumatic Stress in Critical Occupations*. Springfield, IL: Thomas.

McDonald, D.T. (1991) Counselling training for staff in homes for elderly people: problems and possibilities, *Counselling*, 2(1): 12–13.

MacLennan, N. (1996) *Counselling for Managers*. Aldershot: Gower.

McLeod, J. (1998) *An Introduction to Counselling*, 2nd edn. Buckingham: Open University Press.

Macwhinnie, L. (1998) *An Anthology of Counselling at Work*. Rugby: Association for Counselling at Work.

Madden, R.G. (1998) *Legal Issues in Social Work, Counselling and Mental Health*. Thousand Oaks, CA: Sage.

Martin, P. (1997) Counselling skills training for managers in the public sector, in M. Carroll and M. Walton (eds) *Handbook of Counselling in Organisations*. London: Sage.

Masson, J.F. (1988) *Against Therapy: Emotional Tyranny and the Myth of Psychological Healing*. New York: Atheneum.

Megranahan, M. (1994) Counselling in the workplace, in W. Dryden, D. Charles-Edwards and R. Woolfe (eds) *Handbook of Counselling in Britain*. London: Routledge.

Meier, S.T. and Davis, S.R. (1997) *The Elements of Counseling*. Pacific Grove, CA: Brooks/Cole.

Miletich, J.J. (1990) Police, firefighter and paramedic stress, in *An Annotated Bibliography, Bibliographies and Indexes in Psychology*. New York: Greenwood Press.

Mitchell, J.T. (1986) Living dangerously: why firefighters take risks, *Firehouse*, 11: 50–1.

Mitchell, J.T. (1987) Effective stress control at major incidents, *Maryland Fire and Rescue Bulletin*, June: 3–6.

Mitchell, J. and Bray, G. (1990) *Emergency Services Stress: Guidelines for Preserving the Health and Careers of Emergency Service Personnel.* Englewood Cliffs, NJ: Prentice Hall.

Mohr, D.C. (1995) Negative outcome in psychotherapy: a critical review, *Clinical Psychology: Science and Practice,* 2(1): 1–27.

Neal, C. and Davies, D. (2000) *Issues in Therapy with Lesbian, Gay, Bisexual and Transgender Clients.* Buckingham: Open University Press.

Nelson-Jones, R. (1996) *Relating Skills.* London: Cassell.

Nelson-Jones, R. (2000) *Introduction to Counselling Skills.* London: Sage.

Newby, T. (1983) Counselling at work – an overview, *Counselling,* 46: 15–18.

Newton, T. (1995) *'Managing' Stress: Emotion and Power at Work.* London: Sage.

Nixon, J. and Carroll, M. (1994) Can a line manager also be a counsellor?, *Employee Counselling Today,* 6(1): 10–15.

Palmer, S. and Dryden, W. (1996) *Stress Management and Counselling: Theory, Practice Research and Methodology.* London: Cassell.

Palmer Barnes, F. (1998) *Complaints and Grievances in Psychotherapy: A Handbook of Ethical Practice.* London: Routledge.

Panting, G.P. and Palmer, R.N. (1992) *Disclosure of Medical Records.* London: Medical Protection Society.

Pearce, B. (1989) Counselling skills in the context of professional and organisational growth, in W. Dryden, D. Charles-Edwards and R. Woolfe (eds) *Handbook of Counselling in Britain.* London: Routledge.

Pederson, P.B. (2000) *Hidden Messages in Culture-Centred Counselling: A Triad Training Model.* London: Sage.

Peters-Bean, K.M. (2000) Sequential Trauma in the Police. Unpublished PhD thesis, Cranfield University, Beds.

Peterson, K.C., Pront, M. and Schwartz, R.A. (1991) *Post-traumatic Stress Disorder: A Clinician's Guide.* London: Plenum Press.

Philips, M.E., Bruehl, S. and Harden, R.N. (1997) Work-related post traumatic stress disorder: use of exposure therapy and work-simulation activities, *American Journal of Occupational Therapy,* 51(8): 696–700.

Pickard, E. (1993) Designing training for counsellors at work, *Counselling at Work,* autumn: 7–8.

Plas, J.N. and Hoover-Dempsey, K.V. (1988) *Working up a Storm: Anger, Anxiety, Joy and Tears on the Job – and How to Handle Them.* New York: Norton.

Quick, E.K. (1996) *Doing What Works in Brief Therapy: A Strategic Solution Focused Approach.* London: Academic Press.

Raphael, B. and Wilson, J.P. (1994) When disaster strikes: managing emotional reactions in rescue workers, in J.P. Wilson and J.D. Lindy (eds) *Countertransference in the treatment of PTSD.* New York: Guilford Press.

Ravenscroft, T. (1993) Report of a thesis into Post Traumatic Stress Disorder in the London Ambulance Service. Unpublished BAC project, London University.

Reddy, M. (1985) *Counselling Practices Survey*. Milton Keynes: ICAS (Independent Counselling Advisory Service).

Reddy, M. (1994) *The Manager's Guide to Counselling at Work*. London: Methuen.

Reese, J.T., Horn, J.M. and Dunning, C. (eds) (1990) *Critical Incidents in Policing*. Washington, DC: Federal Bureau of Investigation.

Reid, B.R. (1986) *Confidentiality and the Law*. London: Waterloo.

Robinson, R. (1984) Health and Stress in Ambulance Services, report of evaluation study, Part 1, unpublished research project. Victoria, Australia: Social Biology Resource Centre.

Rogers, C.R. (1980) *A Way of Being*. Boston, MA: Houghton Mifflin.

Ross, R.R. and Altmeier, E.M. (1994) *Intervention in Occupational Stress: A Handbook of Counselling for Stress at Work*. London: Sage.

Roy, M.P. and Steptoe, A. (1994) Daily stressors and social support availability as predictors of depressed mood in male firefighters, *Work and Stress*, 8(3): 210–19.

Scott, M. and Stradling, S. (1992) *Counselling for Post Traumatic Stress Disorder*. London: Sage.

Scott, M.J. and Palmer, S. (2000) *Trauma and Post Traumatic Stress Disorder*. London: Cassell.

Scott, N.E. and Borodovsky, L.G. (1990) Effective use of cultural role taking, *Professional Psychology: Research and Practice*, 21(3): 167–70.

Seligman, M. (1995) The effectiveness of psychotherapy: the Consumer Reports study, *American Psychologist*, 50(12): 965–74.

Sills, C. (1997) *Contracts in Counselling*. London: Sage.

Snyder, C.R. and Higgins, R.L. (1988) Excuses: their effective role in the negotiation of reality, *Psychological Bulletin*, 104: 23–35.

Soloman, R.M. (1990) The dynamics of fear in critical incidents: implications for training and treatment, in J.T. Reese, J.M. Horn and C. Dunning (eds) *Critical Incidents in Policing*. Washington, DC: Federal Bureau of Investigation.

Soloman, S.D., Wilson, J. and Keane, T.M. (1997) *Assessing Psychological Trauma and PTSD*. New York: Guilford Press.

Stein, J.H. (1977) Better services for crime victims: a perspective package. *LGAA Grant Report*. Blackstone Institute.

Stewart, W. (1979) *Health Services Counselling*. Tunbridge Wells: Pitman Medical.

Sue, D.W. (1990) Culture-specific strategies in counselling: a conceptual framework, *Professional Psychology: Research and Practice*, 21(6): 424–33.

Tehrani, N. (1998) Does debriefing harm victims of trauma? *Counselling Psychology Review*, 13(3): 6–12.

Thomas, A.M. and Kitzinger, C. (eds) (1997) *Sexual Harassment.* Buckingham: Open University Press.

Thompson, J. and Suzuki, I. (1991) Stress in ambulance workers, *Disaster Management*, 3(4): 193–7.

Toates, F. (1995) *Stress: Conceptual and Biological Aspects.* Chichester: Wiley.

Tyler, G. and Leather, P. (1999) Personality, general well-being and post traumatic stress disorder in the ambulance service, *Occupational Psychologist*, 37: 30–5.

Van der Kolk, B.A., McFarlane, A.C. and Weisaeth, L. (eds) (1996) *Traumatic Stress: The Effects of Overwhelming Experience on Mind, Body, and Society.* New York: Guilford Press.

Walker, M. (1990) *Women in Therapy and Counselling.* Buckingham: Open University Press.

Warr, P. (1987) *Work, Unemployment and Mental Health.* Oxford: Oxford Scientific Publications.

Weiner, M.F. (1983) *Therapist Self-disclosure: The Use of Self in Psychotherapy*, 2nd edn. Baltimore, MD: University Park Press.

Weinrach, S.G. and Thomas, K.R. (1996) The counselling profession's commitment to diversity-sensitive counselling: a critical reassessment, *Journal of Counselling and Development*, 74: 472–7.

Williams, B. (1996) *Counselling in Criminal Justice.* Buckingham: Open University Press.

Woolfe, R. and Dryden, W. (eds) (1996) *Handbook of Counselling Psychology.* London: Sage.

Young, K.M. and Cooper, C.L. (1995) Occupational stress in the ambulance service: a diagnostic study, *Journal of Managerial Psychology*, 12(3): 29–36.

Yule, W. (ed.) (1999) *Post Traumatic Stress Disorders: Concepts and Therapy.* Chichester: Wiley.

Index

THEORY AND PRACTICE IN HUMAN SERVICES

Neil Thompson

This is a revised edition of *Theory and Practice in Health and Social Welfare* which was well received on its first publication:

> Throughout the book the writing is stimulating and thought provoking. The author repeatedly demonstrates a good capacity for synthesizing and summarizing in an accessible manner a range of material which is drawn from many sources . . . encourages the critical questioning that is vitally necessary for those practitioners, educators and trainers who struggle with the elusive and demanding topic of linking theory and practice as a significant part of their working lives.
> *British Journal of Social Work*

> . . . a substantial contribution to the demystification of theoretical and practical issues surrounding health and social welfare.
> *Nursing Times*

Relating theory to practice is a long-standing concern in the human services. This book offers an integrated approach, arguing that theory should be demystified and made relevant to practice, and conversely that practice should be informed by theory in an open, non-dogmatic way.

Readers of the first edition found that it helped them to appreciate the complexities of many of the key issues surrounding the integration of theory and practice. This revised and updated edition covers the latest developments in the relationship between theory and practice. It also contains additional features to aid learning, including a glossary and self-test questions.

The altered title reflects the widened focus of the book which now considers not just social work and social care, nursing and healthcare, but also areas such as probation and community justice, youth and community work, counselling, advocacy and advice work. If you are a student or a practitioner in any of these areas, *Theory and Practice in Human Services* is a book that will encourage you to engage in a process of continuous learning and development, leading to improved practice and increased job satisfaction.

Contents
Introduction – Theory and practice: thinking and doing – What is theory – Science and research – The philosophical basis – Narrowing the gap – Education and training: human resource development – The adventure of theory – Glossary – References – Index.

192pp   0 335 20425 2 (Paperback)   0 335 20426 0 (Hardback)

COUNSELLING SKILLS FOR DOCTORS

Sam Smith and Kingsley Norton

- What are intrinsic counselling skills?
- How can doctors deploy them to help optimize the outcomes of clinical transactions with their patients?
- Can such skills be taught and learned?

This book is about the doctor-patient relationship. It is not about counselling *per se* but about certain counselling skills intrinsic to the medical consultation or clinical transaction. Together with other clinical skills, intrinsic counselling skills are needed to achieve clinical goals, satisfactory to both patient and doctor and appropriate to the clinical transaction and to the wider systems of healthcare.

Clinical transactions can be intellectually, emotionally and sometimes physically demanding. Success depends on doctor and patient adequately fulfilling the obligations and responsibilities of their respective roles. But evidence shows that success also depends on doctors and patients forming a personal relationship of a quality capable of sustaining the sometimes arduous an distressing clinical work. Such a relationship depends on good communication, adequate mutual trust and the ability of doctors to empathize sufficiently with patients and their predicaments. Intrinsic counselling skills are those deployed in the essential task of harmonizing professional and interpersonal aspects of the clinical transaction.

This book is recommended reading for doctors and medical students, post-registration vocational trainees and medical educators within medical schools.

Contents
Introduction – Consulting skills – Intrinsic counselling skills and the clinical transaction – Making a diagnosis: examination and investigation – Managing the problem – Health promotion – Clinical teams and systems of health care – Implications for training – Closing comments – References – Index.

144pp   0 335 20014 1 (Paperback)   0 335 20015 X (Hardback)

COUNSELLING IN MEDICAL SETTINGS

Patricia East

Fundamental changes in the management and delivery of health and community care have resulted from recent government initiatives. At the same time the complex personal relationship between physical, social, environmental and emotional aspects of illness is increasingly being recognized in medical settings. Many claims have been made to justify an expansion of counselling in medical settings as a response to these changes, not only as a supportive therapeutic experience but also as a healing process in its own right. This timely book describes the emergence and growth of counselling in medical settings and examines the issues surrounding its incorporation into this context. Written in a clear accessible style it provides not only a broad overview of counselling and counselling skills but also focuses on specific issues pertinent to counsellors from a wide variety of medical backgrounds. Patricia East's account of counselling in medical settings and the meaning of illness for individuals is enlivened by the extensive use of examples and case material from practitioners.

Contents
The development of counselling in medical settings – Counselling in medical settings – The practice of counselling in medical settings – Specific issues in counselling in medical settings – Professional relationships in counselling in medical settings – A critique of counselling in medical settings – References – Index.

168pp   0 335 19241 6 (Paperback)